VINTAGE LIGHTING

NEW LOCATION

ARCHITECTURAL —ANTIQUES—

An eclectic array of antique & reproduction home accessories and fixtures

356 Richmond Road, Ottawa, K2A 0E8

613-722-1510

Great Books for Collectors!

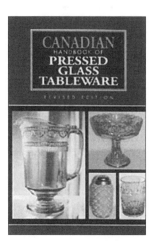

**The Canadian Handbook of
Pressed Glass Tableware**
1-55041-384-8 $39.95

Unitt's Bottles & Values & More
1-55041-205-1 $23.95

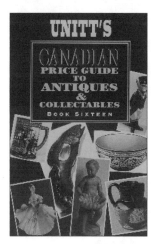

**Unitt's Canadian Price Guide
to Antiques & Collectables 16**
1-55041-185-3 $23.95

**Unitt's Canadian Price
Guide to Dolls & Toys**
1-55041-029-6 $23.95

Fitzhenry & Whiteside
195 Allstate Parkway Markham, Ontario L3R 4T8
Tel: (905) 477-9700   Fax: (905) 477-9179

"FIXTURES PAST & PRESENT"

- Antique claw foot and pedestal tubs
- Embossed toilet bowls and bathroom basins
- Ornate cast iron radiators
- Marble vanity tops with basins and solid brass legs
- Hot water radiators

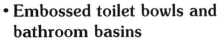

- Porcelain escutheons and handles
- Extensive collection of antique faucets, parts and fittings
- Architectural antiques
- Restoration and repairs
- Prop rentals

Reproduction fixtures and faucets are also available

Call or visit our Showroom

ADDISON'S INC.

41 Wabash Avenue, Toronto, Ontario M6N 1N1
Tel: 416-539-0612 Fax: 416-539-9144
Open 8:00 a.m. to 6:00 p.m. Mon. to Fri.
9:00 a.m. to 5:00 p.m. Saturday

Licenced Master Plumbers

THE MANY FACES OF ANTIQUES IN THIS DAY AND AGE

by Barbara Sutton-Smith

If one of your favourite pastimes is visiting antique shops and shows, which is now possible all year round, then you join millions of others who enjoy the same hobby. They call it a contagious disease.

People looking for antiques in Ontario in the last 35 years have found one of the best tools to be the *Antique Showcase Directory*. This guide to the shops, markets, shows and services has grown enormously since its inception and has proved invaluable for planning antiquing trips or finding shops, some in hidden out of the way places, when in unfamiliar parts of the province. Because it is published bi-annually and kept strictly up-to-date it keeps pace with the changes and movements affecting the Ontario antiques scene. And there have been many changes through the years affecting not only here but 'antiques' practically the world over.

Let's take a look at how this has evolved and become part of today's leisure scene. Probably the most popular event to arrive on the scene in recent years is the one day outdoor shows. Mostly held in the months of May to September this type of informal exhibiting offers an incredibly wide range of things from the past. Not necessarily genuine antiques, but those things we grew up with and have no idea as to what happened to them, or those things we remember so well in Grandma's house, and oh so many things. Obviously weather has a great impact on shows of this nature. Dealers take a considerable risk in hauling everything into the open, and for days before the event watch the weather forecasts most avidly. The promise of a warm, sunny day brings the crowds out in droves and with luck can be a big heyday for dealers.

At these open air shows you trek through parklands or fields and see hundreds, even thousands in some countries, (these are usually several day shows) of dealers offering almost every imaginable thing ever made in times past. Things old and not so old, in good or 'as found' condition, and if luck be with you, you may discover a treasure you can't live without at a bargain price! Although these are fun shows and offer a great relaxing, stress reduced day out, a word of caution is in order 'Caveat Emptor,' 'Buyer Beware.'

In Canada these outdoor shows usually have up to 300 dealers, in the U.S.A. they can go from a few hundred to a few thousand, and in Britain the internationally known Newark show, the largest of them all, boasts 6,000, from well set-up booths to car boots.

The world of antiques as we know them today hasn't always been this way. We have only to turn the clock back 50 years (1950) to know that antique shows were still something of the future, that shops advertising 'Antiques' still followed the hallowed tradition of selling things made at least 100 years earlier (usually much more), these were followed by curiosity or curio and bric-a-brac shops filled with things mostly Victorian – certainly not called antiques at that time, and following on those came the second hand stores handling 20th century or modern domestic household discards.

As for antique shows, apart from private exhibits only the prestigious British Antique Dealer' Fair held at Grosvenor House, Park Lane, London existed. First established in 1934 under the royal patronage of H.M. Queen Mary, discontinued during the war years and re-instituted after, it remains the most famous of all antique shows today. It was also the first fair to institute vetting of every item shown.

By 1951 a few other antique shows appeared, all extremely fines ones, but a little more glitzy and eclectic than the stately Grosvenor. Wimodausis, for instance, which appeared around 1953 in Toronto, was one such show. Unlike many today, these were not commercial ventures but to benefit charities or worthy causes. It took well over another decade before the majority of people showed real interest in their heritage or things of the past.

Here in Canada the centennial year of 1967 had an enormous impact. Everybody suddenly became fervently patriotic, and none more so than those who became dedicated collectors of Canadian made country furniture and primitives, now known as Canadiana.

But this wasn't for everybody. Following in the footsteps of a growing U.S. import market of antiques from England, so Canadian wholesalers, budding antique dealers and auctioneers too began importing large quantities of English and European antiques, and sold to a public whose thirst for these treasures was insatiable. Australia too was a beneficiary of this phenomenon. Huge containers filled with antiques were constantly leaving English ports bound for these countries, and each was building up a post-war major industry.

Of necessity, I suppose one can call this a shifting of assets. England, and other European countries needed the money from these exports and the countries importing were creating a market and filling a need. Whatever, business boomed.

In time supply and demand collided. Eighteenth century and earlier things were getting harder to find and prices were escalating. Victorian made furniture and furnishings, which up to then had been scorned, now gained respectability and favour and gradually Edwardian and early 20th century items too became part of the container loads. Not that there was anything wrong with that, but it was around this time – late 1960s that the antique business underwent a massive change, and a whole new era began which has influenced the antique business as a whole.

Things made from the end of the 19th century, basically known as the art nouveau period, and on through the 1920s-'30s art deco era were in great demand. It didn't matter whether it was furniture, art glass, ceramics, jewellery or objects des'Art, they all sold well. The big problem was that they too, with less than 100 years, and some with only 40 to 50 years of life, were being classified as antiques along with their true ancestral pieces. Although this had been a gradual process it was now evident that the world of antiques had become a wilderness. No doubt that Customs & Excise Dept. were the true culprits when they re-classified antiques as being only over 50 years old for import tax purposes. Old time purist antique dealers were shaking their heads and new time dealers were cashing in on this mixed up deviation from what they considered as normal. Since then a whole generation has passed and the shift to and interest in a whole new range of collectables has taken root.

Over the years all this change has given rise to different levels of antique shops and shows. The collectables market, as it is known in the trade, has been absorbed and become part of the antique scene. Not appreciated by all, but nevertheless a fact of life. Dealers continue to deal in their own particular fields, and the public, although it often follows the route of fashionable trends in antique collecting, appreciates the fact that they can choose a collecting hobby from a much wider field than ever before.

We, like many other countries, still have shops that offer upscale antiques, but the majority, and there are many, many more than 50 years ago, offer a more general line with a high proportion being from sometime in this century. Shows too run from very elegant to very general. In other words there is something for everyone.

Co-op markets have been around for some time, but in the past few years there has been a much greater proliferation of such establishments. Like shows they bring a number of dealers together under one roof. Their trend is more towards collectables and trendy lines.

With all these different ways of marketing 'Antiques' the following guide will help to identify the many different types of venues, where, other than shops, which you can read about in the displays and listings in this book, you can pursue this contagious disease.

Upscale – A high-end show, usually with a benefit night

Offers top quality and rare one-of-a-kind pieces. Often a panel of judges drawn from experts vet the show and guarantees authenticity of age and description. Only the best is seen at these shows. Prices begin around $100 rising to several thousands, and at some top shows can go into millions.

- Venues: Hotel ballrooms, Convention Centres, Armories.
- Dealers: From 30+. Top shows average 85.
- Admission Fee.

Good Quality Conventional Type Show

Professional organizations sponsor these as major charity fund raisers. Commercial promoters also organize this type of show with select dealers offering a diverse, good quality range. Trade advertising often lists names of participating dealers – a clue to the type of show to expect. They do attract more serious collectors because of the wide range of higher calibre decorative arts and furnishings.

- Venues: Mostly Arenas, Church halls, Schools, Convention Centres and any spacious halls.
- Dealers: 30-65
- Admission Fee.

Mall Shows

Most people in Canada are familiar with this style of shopping for antiques. Some promoters and dealers travel a circuit of malls. Booths set up in the centre aisles offer mostly early- to mid-20th century made things in a wide range. Anything from jewellery to furniture dealers. Yorkdale and Sherway are the longest running and most popular. Bayview, the first Sunday in the month except summer is a favourite.

- Dealers: Can range from as few as 15 to as many as 100.

Speciality Shows

Some categories of antiques and collectables have their own specialty shows and each attracts its own dedicated dealers and seasoned collectors. Vintage clothing, toys, tools, postcards, Depression glass, dolls and decoys are just some of the Canadian ones. The number of dealers is often small, perhaps 15-20, but they search for and bring the best available each time. These are usually held annually.

Venue: Small halls
Dealers: 15-20+
Admission Fee.

Nostalgia or Memorabilia Shows

Much of this falls into the collectables bracket. Nostalgia is largely classified as things your Grandmother, or at least her generation (unless dear reader you are an advanced senior citizen), all things to do with that era's homemaking tend to come under this umbrella.

Memorabilia, a subtle difference here. These are things you remember having as a child – and probably wonder what happened to them. You are often tempted to buy back your childhood. Mickey Mouse, Barbie dolls, Dinky & Corgi cars, Leggo, transistor radios, space-age toys are just a few reminders to send your mind whirling back to those tender years. These type of shows have a great following from the baby boomer + crowd.

- Venue: Arenas or small halls
- Dealers: 35+
- Admission Fee.

Outdoor Shows

Held in fields, conservation grounds or parklands. Can run from 100 dealers to thousands. Usually one, but can be two or more day events. Dealers often erect personal tents. An easy, happy atmosphere prevails.

Because of the huge, diverse amount of items available, these shows attract seasoned dealers and collectors looking for their particlar specialties. The general public with a marginal interest in antiques make these events into a day's outing, taking along a picnic lunch. To enjoy these days to the full, a warm sunny day is best. Don't forget your sunscreen and hat!

- Admission Fee.

Flea Markets

Included because you never know what bargains from the past you may find that will be useful. Mostly rated second hand but you will find vintage to new jewellery, china, lamps, magazines, old records, music, recent '50s, '60s, '70s stuff so popular with present day youth "Cool stuff, as they say."

NORTHERN TIME INC.
CANADA'S LEADING BUYER OF FINE WRISTWATCHES

OF INTEREST ARE:

Rolex	Patek Phillipe	LeCoultre	Gublin	Cartier
Vacheron	Movado	Audemars	International	and more . . .

We are placing Wristwatches directly with collectors in Europe and the Orient.
So before you undersell your fine timepiece to the local market, call us for the real value of your product.

**Call (416) 323-1905 Day or Evening, Fax (416) 323-9785
or Write: STEVEN OLTUSKI, 238 Davenport Road, Ste. 292,
Toronto, Ontario M5S 2T2**

Antique
Showcase

2000-2001 Edition

Peter A. sutton-Smith • Publisher

Barbara D. Sutton-Smith • Copy Editor

Copyright©2000. All rights reserved.

ART DIRECTOR: *Janet Coles*
ADVERTISING COMPOSITION AND DESIGN:
*Mary-Anne Luzba, Jim Szeplaki,
Sylvie Tremblay, Cheryl Venneri*

The Antique Showcase Directory Editorial Offices
P.O. Box 70, Brechin, Ontario L0K 1B0
Telephone (705) 484-1668 Fax: (705) 484-1681
Second Class Mail Registraton No. 0017
ISBN – 1-550-41 476-3
The Directory is distributed in conjunction with Fitzhenry & Whiteside, 195 Allstate Parkway, Markham, Ontario L3R 4T8,
(905) 477-9700

ON THE COVER:

IN THIS ISSUE...

INDEX OF TOWNS

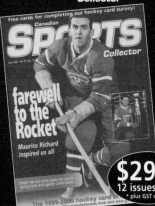

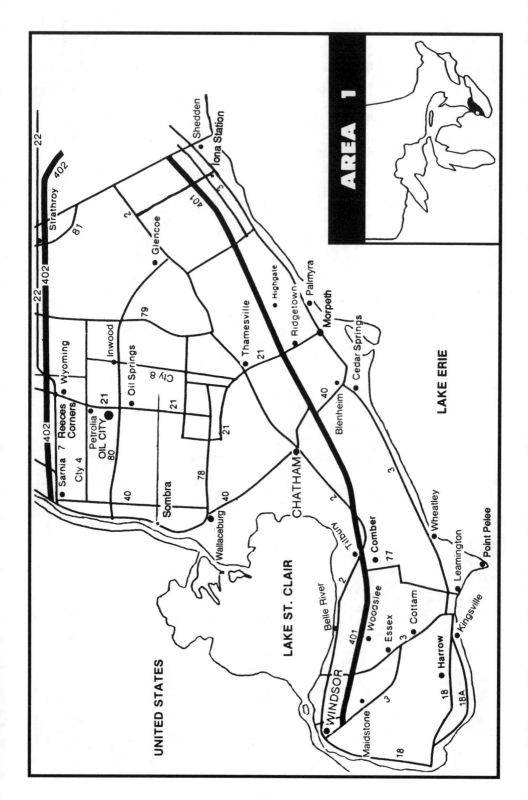

BELLE RIVER
FERN & LINDA'S
1537 Hwy. 2, R.R. #3
519-727-6710   N0R 1A0
10-5 Open daily, closed Wednesday.
Furniture, Antiques & Collectibles.

BLENHEIM
JOHNSON'S ANTIQUES
8094 Talbot Trail   N0P 1A0
3 miles w. of Blenheim on Hwy. 3
Sally Johnson
519-676-8565
Open all year, most afternoons.
Quality antique Canadian
Furniture & smalls.

CEDAR SPRINGS
KEN'S ANTIQUES
Water Street (Rifle Range Rd.)
Ken Lucio   N0P 1K0
519-676-8185
Open by chance or appointment.
General line of antiques.
Household auctions
Every Thursday at 7 p.m.

CHATHAM
ANTIQUE SHOW & SALE
Kinsmen Auditorium Community Centre
Kent Regiment Chapter IODE
Held annually on first
Weekend in May.
Check monthly
Showcase for dates.

CHATHAM
DOROTHY'S COUNTRY ANTIQUES
Hwy. #40   N7M 5J3
North of 401 overpass
Dorothy Fox
519-352-0037
Open Wednesday thru Sunday (afternoons).
Furniture, glass,
China & collectibles.

CHATHAM
THERESA'S WOOD SHED
137 St. Clair Street   N8L 2J2
Theresa Myers
2 Blks. N. of Hwy. 2 on 40 Hwy.
519-352-8982 or 352-7587
10-5:30 Tuesday thru Saturday,
11-5 on Sunday.
Refinishing, woodworking,
Furniture, glass & china.

GLENCOE
THE HITCHING POST
Main Street   N0L 1M0
Jim & Carol Grover
519-693-4935
10-4 Monday thru Saturday,
Closed Wednesday.
Furniture, glass, pottery,
Prints, Primitives,
& Hooked Rugs.

HIGHGATE – PALMYRA
SPRINGRIDGE ANTIQUES
1 Km. N. of #3 Hwy. on Highgate Rd.
Jean & Jim Gillard
519-674-3546
Open most days year round.
Oil lamps, quilts,
Farm tools, primitives,
Glass, furniture,
Kitchen collectibles & china.

IONA
IONA COMMONS GENERAL
1 Blk. south of Hwy. 3   N0L 1P0
Wayne & Cindy Irwin
519-764-2662
Open daily year round.
Furniture, pottery,
Primitives and
Canadian folk art.

IONA STATION
SHAUNESSY ANTIQUES
R.R. #3   N0L 1P0
7th Concession – 1st house on right
between Iona Station & Iona.
Doreen & Jack Shaunessy
519-762-5885
Open by chance or appointment.
Quality refinished
Furniture & accessories.

CARING FOR ANTIQUE FURNITURE

• Period furniture should never be placed close to central heating radiators or any other source of direct heat, as this can lead to veneers lifting and joints drying out. Damage caused in this way should not be blamed on the person you bought the furniture from. If you have many fine early pieces it is advisable to invest in a good humidifier, either the free-standing electric type that uses several pints of water a day, or one that can be plumbed-in permanently in a central position in the house.

• Do not over-polish furniture; too much wax polish can become sticky. A dining table in daily use should perhaps be wax polished every other week, but for other items, such as bureaux and book-cases, three or four times a year (with occasional rubs with a dry duster) should be enough. Use only reputable wax polish from a tin or jar, not aerosol sprays. A 50/50 mixture of vinegar and water is a good cleaner if a dining table gets greasy or sticky. Rub dry and wax sparingly.

• When deciding to re-upholster or re-cover period furniture, choose a pattern that goes well with your colour scheme rather than worrying about what the original fabric might have looked like; a good design sense is more important than hard and fast rules.

• Drawers that do not run well can be eased by rubbing a piece of wax candle lightly along the friction parts, i.e. runners and sides.

• Serious water or heat marks on table surfaces should only be dealt with by a professional polisher, but very light marks can sometimes be removed with fine steel wool (gauge 0000) and then burnished gently with Brasso metal polish to match the surrounding shine.

• If pieces of inlay or veneer come off when e.g. dusting furniture, be sure to keep them, however small. They will save hours of restorer's time – and money!

• Brass inlay on furniture is prone to "springing" out. Do not blame the person you bought the item from – it is usually the result of changes in temperature and humidity that cause the timber to expand or contract. All you can do is to tape the loose end of the inlay down until it can be dealt with by a competent restorer.

• Avoid pulling small tables across a carpet on their castors, as this causes enormous strain in the leg joints – lift them.

• Regard your fine furniture as something requiring maintenance, like your house and your car, and get a good professional restorer to look it over every few years. In this way you will minimize the amount of major (and costly) work to be done in the long run.

• Patina: that lovely soft glow that can only result from the effect of gentle polishing, light and loving care over many years, is precious. Never remove it, except in cases where a surface is so badly disfigured that you cannot bear to live with it.

KINGSVILLE
THERE'S NO PLACE LIKE HOME
2092 Division Street North   N9Y 2Z3
M. Reynolds, P. Vandenberg
519-733-8029
Wednesday thru Saturday, 12-5
Antiques & collectibles.
Specializing in gramophones,
Victorian, glass, china &
Costume jewellery.

LEAMINGTON
POINT PELEE ANTIQUE PLACE
617 Point Pelee Drive, R.R. #1   N9H 3V4
Joyce Perry Simard
519-326-6517
Summer: Fri., Sat., Sun., noon-4 p.m.
Winter: By chance or appointment.
Antiques, collectibles,
Jewellery, old dolls
& Primitives.

LEAMINGTON
ANTIQUE SHOW & SALE
The Roma club
Balmoral Chapter IODE
Held annually in April.
Check monthly
Showcase for dates.

MORPETH
GEORGIAN HOUSE ANTIQUES
6 Main Street   N0P 1X0
Junaito Agustin
Frederick Smith
519-674-0418
Open most days,
Or by chance.
Fine art & antiques.

PETROLIA
NEMO HALL ANTIQUES
419 King Street   N0N 1R0
Lola Martel
519-882-0436
10-6, Thursday thru Sunday.
For other times please phone.
Furniture, glass, crystal, brass,
Porcelain, etc.
"Something for everyone."

RIDGETOWN
ANTIQUE SHOW & SALE
RIDGETOWN HIGH SCHOOL
Off Main Street E.
Ridgetown Rotary Club
Held annually
On 1st or 2nd weekend of July.
Info: 519-674-2955
Check monthly
Showcase for dates.

SARNIA
ANNE-TIQUES
MACKLIN'S FLOWERS
149 North Mitton Street   N7T 6G9
3 blocks south of Sarnia Hospital
Anne & Vic Tarr
519-337-2392
9-5:30 Monday thru Saturday,
9-3 Wednesday. Closed Sunday.
China, collectables, silver, linen,
Olde lace, books & kitchenware.

STRATHROY
CLARK'S ANTIQUE SPECIALTY
SUPPLY LTD.
P.O. Box 73   M7G 3J1
Lavarre and Scott Clark
519-245-9838
Toll free: 1-877-689-7811
Mail order service.
Refinishing products, antique restoration.
Hardware & specialty supplies.

WHEATLEY
THE OLD LOG HOUSE
Hwy. #3, 108 Talbot East
P.O. Box 141   N0P 2P0
Pat Alton
519-825-7783
9:30-5 Monday thru Friday,
10-5 Saturday, 12-4 Sunday.
Antiques, collectibles
& Primitives.

WINDSOR
THE OLDE SHOPPE
134 Hanna Street West   N8X 1E1
Felix Wagner
519-254-7225
9-5:30 Monday thru Friday, 9-5 Saturday.
Closed Sunday.
Fine antiques, gold & silver jewellery,
Glass, china, sterling silver.
Estate & insurance appraisals.

ANTIQUE FURNITURE

PERIODS	TUDOR		STUART		RESTORATION	
STYLE {	ELIZABETHAN	JACOBEAN	CROMWELLIAN	CAROLEAN		WILLIAM & MARY
	1558-1603	1603-1649	1649-1660	1660-1689		1689-1702
WOODS		O A K			W A L N U T	

1570 1570 1590 1600 1610 1620 1630 1640 1650 1660 1670 1680 1690 1700

CHAIR LEGS

CHAIR BACKS

CARVING & ORNAMENT

METAL-WORK

RECOGNITION CHART

Q. ANNE		GEORGIAN						VICTORIAN
QUEEN ANNE 1702-1714	EARLY GEORGIAN 1714-1745	CHIPPEN-DALE 1745-1780	ADAM 1758-1792	HEPPLE-WHITE 1760-1790	SHERATON 1790-1810	FRENCH EMPIRE 1793-1830	REGENCY 1830-1837	EARLY VICTORIAN 1837-1850

WALNUT   MAHOGANY   (SATINWOOD)

1700 1710 1720 1730 1740 1750 1760 1770 1780 1790 1800 1810 1820 1830 1840 1850

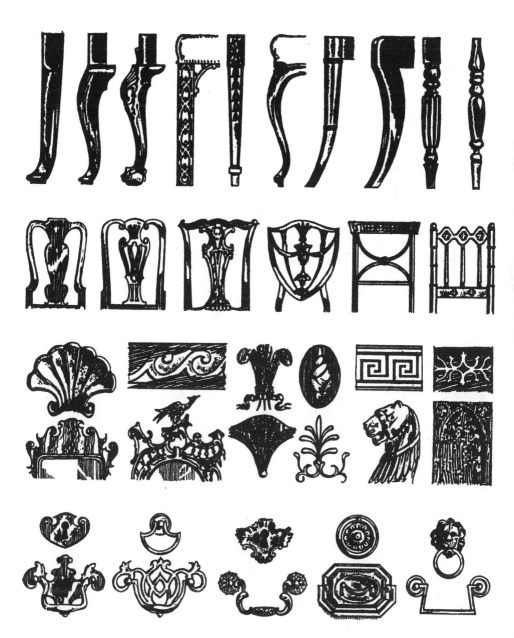

- 21 -

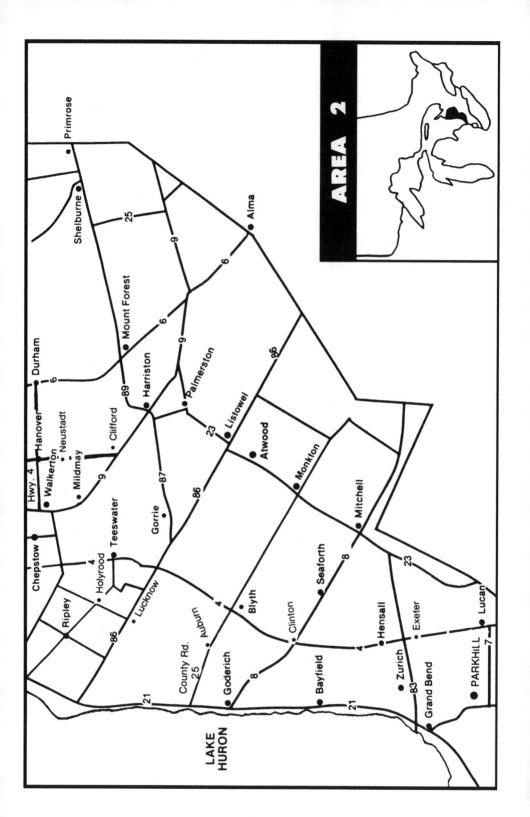

AREA 2

Primrose
Shelburne
25
9
Alma
6
Mount Forest
6
9
Durham
6
Harriston
Palmerston
86
Hanover
Hwy. 4
Neustadt
Clifford
89
23
Listowel
Atwood
Walkerton
Mildmay
9
87
Gorrie
86
Monkton
Mitchell
Chepstow
Teeswater
Seaforth
8
4
Holyrood
Lucknow
Blyth
23
Ripley
86
Clinton
Hensall
Exeter
Lucan
County Rd.
25
Auburn
4
Zurich
PARKHILL
7
Goderich
8
Bayfield
83
21
21
Grand Bend
LAKE
HURON

BLYTH
REMEMBER WHEN...
170 Dinsley Street West   N0M 1H0
Elaine Scrimgeour
519-523-9554
Mon.-Sat. from 10-8, June 30th to mid-Sept.
Other times by chance or appointment.
Antiques & collectibles.
Also new accents to complement decor
From Victorian to country.

CARLOW
CARLOW GENERAL STORE
Turn east off Hwy. #21 on to
The Blythe Road (go 4 km.)
519-524-6166
Open year round – 7 days
6-6 Monday thru Thursday,
6-8 Friday, 10-6 weekends.
Antiques & nostalgia from 1800s
Through to 1950s, '60s and '70s.

EXETER
C.R. CORNISH ANTIQUES
P.O. Box 88   N0M 1S6
519-235-0296
Exhibiting at major shows.
Fine quality glass & china,
Silver & small furniture.

HANOVER
CAMPBELL'S CORNER
CONSIGNMENT SHOP
893 10th Street   N4N 1S4
Doloras Shiel
519-364-1444
Open daily except Mondays.
Closed Sundays in July & August.
Antiques, collectibles, quality used clothing, furniture.

HANOVER
DEFINITELY DENNIS
269 10th Street   N4N 1P1
Dennis Agombar
519-364-1331
Open daily, 10:30-6,
Sunday 1-5.
Jewellery, militaria, novelties, stamps,
Coins, books, collectibles.
"We may be small but we're filled wall to wall."

HARRISTON
DAVIES ANTIQUES and FLEA MARKET
43 Elora Street   N0G 1Z0
519-338-2449
9-5 daily.
Nippon & Depression glass,
Furniture and primitives.
Also at 64 Raglan St.,
By chance or appointment.

HENSALL
PETER & JANIS BISBACK ANTIQUES
88 Queen Street East   N0M 1X0
2 Blocks west of Hwy. #4
519-262-3505
Open all year.
By chance or appointment.
Specializing in early
Canadian furniture & folk art.

ZURICH
THE PIGEON LOFT
36 Goshen Street North   N0M 2T0
Mrs. Lois Thiel
519-236-4983
By appointment.
Large diversified stock.
Lamps and pressed glass.

MARKS ON CONTINENTAL POTTERY AND PORCELAIN

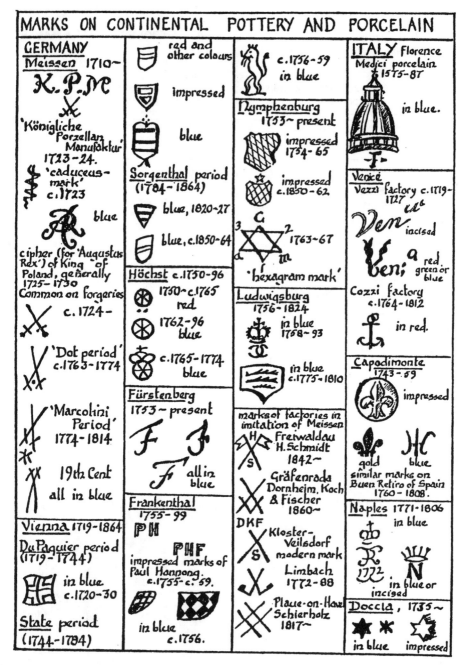

GERMANY
Meissen 1710~

K.P.M

'Königliche Porzellan Manufaktur' 1723-24.

'caduceus-mark' c.1723

blue

cipher (for 'Augustus Rex') of King of Poland, generally 1725-1730. Common on forgeries

c.1724~

'Dot period' c.1763-1774

'Marcolini Period' 1774-1814

19th Cent all in blue

Vienna 1719-1864

Du Paquier period (1719-1744)

in blue c.1720-30

State period (1744-1784)

---

red and other colours

impressed

blue

Sorgenthal period (1784-1864)

blue, 1820-27

blue, c.1850-64

Höchst c.1750-96

1750~c.1765 red

1762-96 blue

c.1765-1774 blue

Fürstenberg 1753~ present

all in blue

Frankenthal 1755-99

PH

PHF impressed marks of Paul Hannong. c.1755~c.59.

in blue c.1756.

---

c.1756-59 in blue

Nymphenburg 1753~ present

impressed 1754-65

impressed c.1850-62

1763-67 'hexagram mark'

Ludwigsburg 1756-1824

in blue 1758-93

in blue c.1775-1810

marks of factories in imitation of Meissen

Freiwaldau H.Schmidt 1842~

Gräfenroda Dornheim, Koch & Fischer 1860~

DKF

Kloster-Veilsdorf modern mark

Limbach 1772-88

Plaue-on-Havel Schierholz 1817~

ITALY Florence
Medici porcelain 1575-87

in blue.

Venice
Vezzi factory c.1719-1727

incised

red, green or blue

Cozzi factory c.1764-1812

in red.

Capodimonte 1743-59

impressed

gold   blue

similar marks on Buen Retiro of Spain 1760-1808.

Naples 1771-1806

in blue

in blue or incised

Doccia, 1735~

in blue   impressed

The torches of La Courtille, the hooks of Rauenstein, the hayforks of Rudolstadt, the "L"s of Limbach, and the "W" of Wallendorf, were all drawn in such a way as to resemble the Meissen mark.

The firm of Samson & Co. was established in Paris in 1845, claiming to make "Reproductions of Ancient Works emanating from the Museums and from Private Collections." When imitating the true hard-paste porcelain of the Far East or the Continent, Samson's wares are difficult to detect, due to their being made from similar materials, whereas his reproductions of such English factories as Bow, Chelsea, and Derby are more easily recognized as fakes. Unfortunately the range of Samson's marks, illustrated above, do not appear to have been regularly used, or, as is sometimes the case, the original mark has been removed by grinding or by etching away with acid, and a replica of a known genuine mark added.

年洪
製武

Hung Wu
(1368~1398)

德 大
年 明
製 宣

Hsüan Tê
(1426-1435)

In seal characters

化 大
年 明
製 成

Ch'êng Hua
(1465~1487)

In seal characters

慶 大
年 明
製 隆

Lung Ch'ing
(1567~1572)

建文

Chien Wên
(1399~1402)

治 大
年 明
製 弘

Hung Chih
(1488~1505)

曆 大
年 明
製 萬

Wan Li
(1573~1619)

Yung Lo
(1403-1424)
In archaic script

正 統

Chêng T'ung
(1436-1449)

德 大
年 明
製 正

Chêng Tê
(1506~1521)

泰 昌

T'ai Ch'ang (1620)

年 永
製 樂

Yung Lo
(1403~1424)

景 泰

Ching T'ai
(1450~1457)

靖 大
年 明
製 嘉

Chia Ching
(1522~1566)

啟 大
年 明
製 天

T'ien Ch'i
(1621~1627)

洪 熙

Hung Hsi (1425)

天 順

T'ien Shun
(1457~1464)

年 崇
製 楨

Ch'ung Chêng
(1628~1643)

Factory marks in the Western sense are practically unkown on Chinese porcelain wares, while those purporting to record the period of manufacture are so liable to be "commemorative," or even deliberately fraudulent, as to be a frequent cause of dispute among students. Marks of the Ming Chinese Emperors, Hsüan Tê, Ch'êng Hua and Chia Ching are commonly found on wares of the reign of the Ch'ing Emperor K'ang Hsi, while the reign name of K'ang Hsi himself, rare on the abundant porcelain of his period, is chiefly found on 19th- and 20th-century wares.

Under the rule of the Ming Emperors (1368-1644) the Sung ideals in pottery were largely rejected in favour of the vogue for fine-grained white porcelain heralding the beginning of a new period in Chinese ceramic history with its centre in the town of Ching-tê Chên in Kiangsi province where a new Imperial factory was started in 1369 with a prolific output of early Ming blue-and-white

Shun Chih
(1644~1661)

In seal characters

Tao Kuang
(1821~1850)

In seal characters

In seal characters

In seal characters

Ch'ien Lung
(1736-1795)

In seal characters

Kuang Hsü
(1874~1908)

K'ang Hsi
(1662~1722)

In seal characters

Hsien Fêng
(1851~1861)

In seal characters

In seal characters

Chia Ch'ing
(1796~1821)

In seal characters

Hsüan T'ung
(1909~1912)

Yung Chêng
(1723~1735)

In seal characters

T'ung Chih
(1862~1873)

Hung Hsien
(1916)
(Yüan Shih-kai)

and fine enamel-painted porcelain both for the court and later for general use and export.

Following the fall of the Ming Dynasty in 1644 their declining culture was revived by the Ch'ing Emperor K'ang Hsi (1662-1722) who was a great patron of the arts. The European influence of the French and Netherlandish Jesuits at his courts is seen in the Baroque character of the early Ch'ing porcelain.

There was a backward-looking tendency during the reigns of Yung-Chêng (1723-35) and Ch'ien Lung (1736-95) when exact copies of the classical Sung wares and the early Ming painted porcelain were made.

The Imperial porcelain of the 19th century was as a rule carefully and weakly correct in following earlier styles and models. the factory was burnt in 1853 by the Tai-ping rebels and hardly recovered before the 1911 revolution ended the Dynasty.

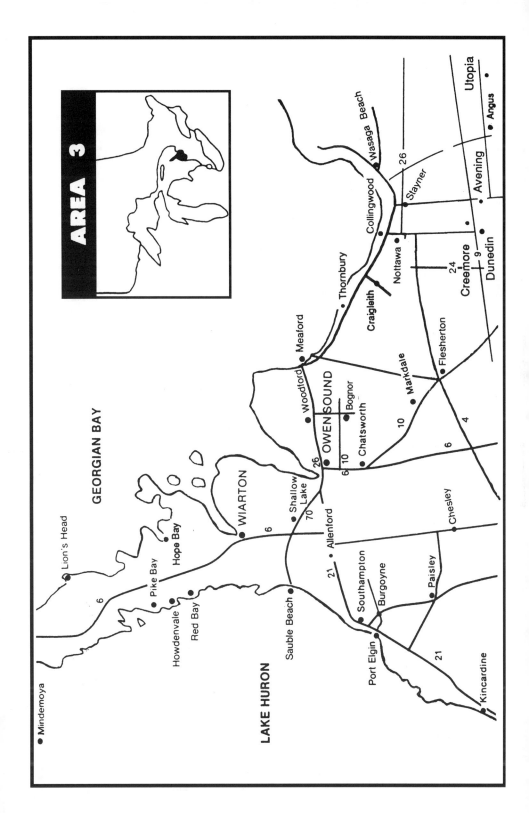

AREA 3

GEORGIAN BAY

LAKE HURON

Mindemoya

Lion's Head

Pike Bay
Howdenvale
Red Bay
Hope Bay

WIARTON

Sauble Beach

Shallow Lake

Southampton
Burgoyne

Port Elgin

Kincardine

Allenford

Paisley

Chesley

OWEN SOUND

Bognor
Chatsworth

Woodford

Markdale

Meaford

Flesherton

Thornbury

Craigleith

Collingwood

Nottawa

Creemore
Dunedin

Stayner

Wasaga Beach

Avening

Angus

Utopia

6
21
21
70
6
26
10
6
10
4
24
9
26
26

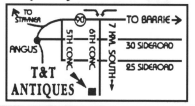

ALLENFORD
THE SHARON SHOP

Hwy. 21, P.O. Box 4   N0H 1A0
Gerry Wright
519-934-2173
Antiques & nostalgia
Including furniture, crocks
Bottles, fruit jars & collectibles.
1st Editions &
Vintage paperbacks.

ANGUS
WAKEFIELD ANTIQUES
& COLLECTABLES

25 Lee Avenue, P.O. Box 369   L0M 1B0
705-424-5465
Marg. & Brian Wakefield
Open by chance or appointment.
Usually open most evenings & weekends.
A call ahead is preferred.
Antique furnishings from Britain.

AVENING
KATHY McCLEARY'S INTERIORS

R.R. #3, Creemore   L0M 1G0
Kathy McCleary
705-466-3019
1 Hr. N. of Toronto on Airport Road
Open weekends.
Weekdays by chance or appointment.
Interior design consultation.
The Antique... The Unique... The Mystique...

AVENING
McCLEARY'S ANTIQUES

R.R. #3, Creemore   L0M 1G0
Richard & Kathy
705-466-3019
1 Hr. N. of Toronto on Airport Road
Open weekends.
Weekdays by chance or appointment.
Canadian country furniture,
Refinished & original finishes.

COLLINGWOOD
THE VILLAGE SHOP

Blue Mountain Rd., across from
Toronto Ski Club, R.R. #3   L9Y 3Z2
Brenda Martinek
705-445-6339
Open weekends from 9-6 or by appointment.
Early Canadian furniture – guaranteed to
Enhance any chalet, house or apartment.
Dealers welcome.

CREEMORE
BELHAVEN ANTIQUES

County Rd. #9 (2 miles W. of Creemore
between Creemore & Dunedin)   L0M 1G0
Lindsay Bell & Wayne Winters
705-466-3368; Fax: 705-466-2781
Summer: Daily 10-5.
Winter: Weekends 10-5
Weekdays by chance.
Antiques of Distinction.

CREEMORE
THE CREEMORE CLOCK COMPANY

148 Mill Street   L0M 1G0
John Durrant
705-466-3152
10-5 Monday thru Thursday, 10-6 Friday,
9-5 Saturday, 12-4 Sunday.
Repairs to all makes & models.
Grandfather clocks a specialty.

FLESHERTON
MARY SARAH ANTIQUES

On Hwy. #4, 1 Block east of Hwy. #10
P.O. Box 247   N0C 1E0
Carolyn Somers
519-924-3206
Open most days all year round.
Specializing in early Canadian pine,
Refinished & original paint. Primitives
And folk art. 3,000 sq. ft. of display.

KINCARDINE
DOUBLE D ENTERPRISES

1148 Queen Street   N2Z 1G5
Don Roberts
519-396-2375
By appointment only.
Refinishing supplies of antiques.
Trade discounts.
Catalogue upon request.
Mail order our specialty.

KINCARDINE
J&B ANTIQUES

93 Goderich Street   N2Z 2K8
Jim Phillips
519-396-8261
Pine, cherry &
Butternut our specialty.
Country, Victorian and
Turn-of-Century
Furnishings.

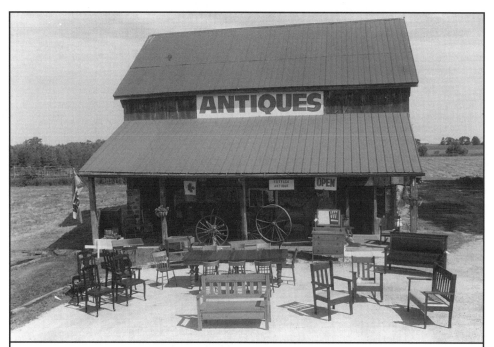

NOTES

MARKDALE
BILL AND MARY'S ANTIQUES

13 Toronto Street South   N0C 1H0
877-986-1311
11-5 Wednesday thru Saturday,
Other times by chance.
Antiques, collectibles & nostalgia.
Depression, Carnival, Pressed & Victorian
Art glass, China, Nippon, R.S., Royal
Doulton, etc., Primitives and collector books.

MARKDALE
MAC'S TIQUES

75 Maint Street West   N0C 1H0
2 Blks. west of Lights
Barb & Ross Macdonald
519-986-2225 or 986-4252
Open daily, 10-5. Sundays from 12-5.
Canadiana, Victoriana, china, glass,
Primitives, nostalgia, collector plates,
Country accessories.

MARKDALE
THE COUNTRY STORE

8 Main Street West   N0C 1H0
Katherine Taylor
519-986-3702
Open 9-5, Tuesday thru Saturday,
Sunday 12-5, or by appointment.
Canadian furniture & accessories.
Folk art & gifts.
Dealers for Sturbridge Village paints.

MEAFORD
POKEABOUT

Harbour Lane
36 Trowbridge Street East, Unit 3 N4L 1G1
Joanna Cole – 519-538-1166
Saturday & Sunday 10:30-5:00
Or by appointment.
Victorian antiques & accessories.

LION'S HEAD
GLORY BE ANTIQUE GLASS

89 Main Street, Box 911   N0H 1W0
Madeline Hewton
519-793-3940
10-5 Daily or by chance.
May 24th Weekend to Thanksgiving.
Hanging lamps, Limoge, Wedgwood,
Pressed glass, Cranberry glass.

MEAFORD
TREASURE CHEST

Harbour Lane
36 Trowbridge Street East   N4L 1G1
519-538-2646 or 538-4658 (res.)
11-5 Thursday thru Sunday.
Specializing in old quilts,
Framed pictures, furniture &
Interesting & unusual items.

TORQUAY POTTERY MARKS

TRADE MARK

Black stamp
Transfer printed
1884-1890

Watcombe
Torquay
England

Incised
1901-1920

WATCOMBE
TORQUAY

Black stamp
1902-1915

WATCOMBE
TORQUAY
MADE IN
ENGLAND

Impressed
1915-1920

WATCOMBE
DEVON
MOTTO
WARE
ENGLAND

Black stamp
1918-1927

ROYAL
WATCOME
TORQUAY
ENGLAND

Black stamp
1935-1962

Impressed
Exeter Art Pottery
1892-1896

H.M.EXETER

Impressed
Hart & Moist
1896-1935

DEVON
TORS
POTTERY

Devon Tors
Impressed
1920-1939

BOVEY TRACEY
ART POTTERY
DEVON

Black stamp
Subsidiary, TPCO
1922-1930

LEMON & CRUTE
TORQUAY

Black stamp
Lemon & Crute
1925-1928

PLYMOUTH
GAS FIRED

Plymouth Pottery
Impressed
1925-1926

TORQUAY POTTERY MARKS

ALLERVALE Serifs Impressed 1885-1893	**ALLER VALE** Impressed 1891-1910	**ALLER VALE HH&CO.** Impressed 1897-1902
Aller Vale **Devon** Black Ink, brush 1902-1924	**LONGPARK TORQUAY** Impressed 1903-1909	*Tormohun Ware* Incised 1903-1914
LONGPARK TORQUAY. Black stamp 1904-1918	**LONG PARK TORQUAY DEVON** Black stamp 1925-1957	 **LIMITED** Black transfer 1875-1890
 **STAPLETON** Impressed 1890-1905	 Brush, black ink 1905-1920	**ROYAL TORQUAY POTTERY ENGLAND** Black stamp 1924-1940

I hunted for it, found it, bought it, washed it, scrubbed it, repaired it, fixed it, patched it, labelled it, catalogued it, framed it, displayed it, bragged about it, paid insurance on it, and sometimes broke it. Now how can I take anything less?

PIKE BAY
LAMPLIGHTER ANTIQUES REG'D
17 Fraser Road.
Mailing: R.R. #1 Mar.   N0H 1X0
Pike Bay is in Bruce Peninsula,
45 miles N.W. of Owen Sound.
Vera C. Fraser, 519-793-3133
By appointment only July & August,
Or by chance.
Lamps, pressed & art glass, large
Diversified stock prior to 1925. 41st Year.

PORT ELGIN
SUNNYHILL FARMS
R.R. #2   N0H 2C0
7 Miles east of Port Elgin on Tara Rd.
Steward & May Esplen
519-389-5210
Open 9-6 daily. Other times by appointment.
Antique china, glass, jewellery,
Furniture "in the rough."
In business for 25 years.

SAUBLE BEACH
GRANNI MAX ANTIQUES
210 Main Street   N0H 2G0
Maxine Thompson
519-422-3159
Open weekends April & May.
Summer months open daily.
Glassware, one-of-a-kind items,
Brass, quality furniture & collectables.

STAYNER
BLUE HOUSE ANTIQUES
Hwy. #26, 2 km. north of Stayner
R.R. #2, P.O. Box 1134, Stayner   L0M 1S0
Bob & Agnes Charlton
705-428-6943
Open most of the time, but a call ahead
Will avoid disappointment.
Country furnishings, quilts & baskets.

STAYNER
COTTAGE ANTIQUES & COLLECTABLES
Hwy. 26 East, Main Street   L0M 1S0
Fay Emerson, 705-428-2768
Summer: Open daily
Winter: If coming a distance
A call ahead is advised.
Specializing in a large selection of
Quality oak, walnut and mahogany furniture.

STAYNER
J.R.'s ANTIQUES
Hwy. 91, 2 km. west of Stayner
Box 1055   L0M 1S0
Alexandra & James Robbinson
705-428-3301
www.JRantiques.com
Open year-round. Closed Wednesday.
Specializing in pine.
1,500 Antique and reproduction
Pieces in stock.

STAYNER
PINE PLUS MIRRORS & ANTIQUES
Elm & Brock Streets, Box 952   L0M 1S0
Barbara Elliott
705-428-6538; 1-877-464-0136
10-5 Daily May thru October,
Wednesdays by chance,
Closed November thru April.
Country furniture, mirrors, glassware,
China, frames, pictures, collectibles.
Dessert Tearoom open same hours.

UTOPIA
T&T ANTIQUES
R.R. #1   L0M 1T0
Barry & Carol Tarling
705-424-7027
Open weekends or
By chance or appointment.
Choice selection of Victorian
Furniture & accessories, china,
Canadian furniture & textiles.

WASAGA BEACH
DEEMAR ANTIQUES
Marcel de Vries
Hwy. #26 at Baysands   L0L 2P9
705-429-6539
Offering a fine selection of
Pine & oak furniture,
Clocks, china & glass.

WIARTON
THE BRUCE BECKONS
R.R. #4 off Hwy. #6
2 Miles north of Wiarton   N0H 2T0
519-534-1256 or 534-3669
Open weekends from Mar. 1 thru Dec. 31.
Open Fri., Sat. & Sun. in July & Aug.
Specializing in primitives &
Pine furniture displayed in a
Century log cabin.

Belhaven Antiques

Antiques of Distinction

Belhaven Antiques is one of Ontario's most distinctive shops. We display an extensive selection of quality antiques, works of art, and decorative pieces, featuring an eclectic mix of formal and country furniture, art glass, signed lamps, jewelry, china, and clocks.

Five showrooms displaying an extensive selection of Quality Antiques and Works of Art
• No Reproductions

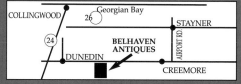

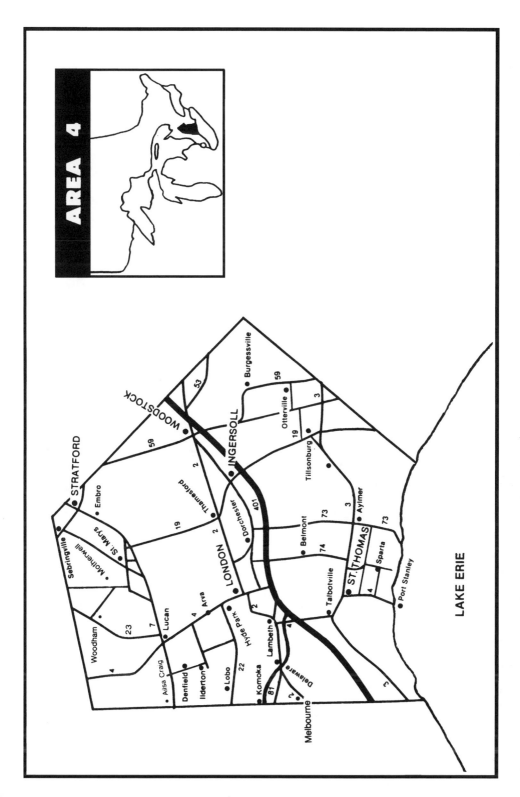

AREA 4

LAKE ERIE

- 39 -

DELAWARE
HILL TOP OLDE TYME MARKET
8898 Longwoods Rd., Hwy. #2   N0L 1E0
2 kms west of Delaware
519-264-9538 or 1-877-278-1373
Open daily year round. Closed Dec. 25
Summer 9-5; Winter 10-5
The Ivy Shoppe, The Paisley Room,
Images of Past. Antiques, collectibles, nostalgia.
Unique & Unusual Gift Ideas,
Country kitchen, Special Events.

DELAWARE
MILL ANTIQUES
R.R. #1   N0L 1E0
Located on Hwy. #2 at the Delaware
Sawmill, 12 miles west of London.
Grace Patrick
519-652-3740
Open daily by chance or appointment.
We buy & sell... Antiques,
Furniture & collectibles.

LAMBETH
GRANNY'S TREASURES
46 Main Street   N0L 1S0
Jane Galbraith
519-652-1090
10-5 Daily,
July & August by chance
Or appointment.
Antiques & collectibles.

LAMBETH
GORDON F. BAKER ANTIQUES
67 Main Street East   N0L 1S0
519-652-9290
10-4 daily, by chance
Or appointment.
Furniture, glass, china,
Paintings, jewellery,
Collectibles, etc.

LONDON
ANTIQUES AT HYDE PARK
1380 Fanshawe Park Rd. W.   N6G 5B1
Just east at Hyde Park
519-472-0322
Fax: 519-472-6175
10-6 Seven days
Thursday & Friday until 9 p.m.
200 Booths of antiques & collectables.

LONDON
ATTIC BOOKS
240 Dundas Street   N6A 1H3
Marvin Post, Nancy Buckingham
519-432-7277
10-5:30 Monday thru Saturday,
Friday until 9 p.m. (April-December),
Closed Sunday.
Fine books:
Bought – Sold – Traded.

LONDON
BAKEROSA
188 Deer Park Circle   N6H 3C1
Art & Sheila Baker
519-472-0827
Phone or mail orders welcome
Or open by chance.
Books & price guides on
Antiques & collectibles. Limited edition
Collector plates. Free list, send SASE.

LONDON
BALL FURNITURE REFINISHING LTD.
380 Spruce Street   N5W 4N7
Jim & Charlaine Martin
519-455-5800
7-4 Monday thru Friday,
By appointment, after hours,
And Saturday & Sunday.
Fine furniture, antiques,
Depression glass, collectables.

LONDON
CITY CENTRE FURNITURE &
ANTIQUES
203 Bathurst Street   N6B 1P1
519-645-7533; Fax: 519-645-2690
9:30-6 Monday thru Saturday
Friday until 9, 12-4:30 Sunday
Antiques and estate furnishings, including art,
Lighting, china, etc., bought and sold.
Furniture refinishing, Luncheons counter.

LONDON
CLARK'S ANTIQUE SPECIALTY
SUPPLY LTD.
Please note change of address.
See Area 1 – Strathroy.
Refinishing products, reproduction
Hardware & specialty supplies.

LONDON
DUMAC ANTIQUES
Jim MacIntyre, Earl Squyre
Tel./Fax: 519-472-4820
At shows or by appointment
Specializing in early porcelain,
Art glass, pottery,
Discontinued China and collectibles.
We buy and collect Carltonware.

LONDON
MEMORY LANE OF HYDE PARK
1175 Hyde Park Road (at Sarnia Rd.) N6H 5K6
519-471-2835, Fax: 519-471-0864
Open seven days,
13,000 Sq. ft. showroom with
95 Discriminating dealers.
Fine china, glass, silver, watches, artware,
Jewellery, clocks, crocks, decoys, nostalgia, etc.,
Quality pine and vintage furniture.

LONDON
FOREST CITY COINS & STAMPS LTD.
354 Richmond Street   N6A 3C3
Keith S. Greenham
519-434-3355
E-mail: keithg@golden.net
10-5:30 Monday thru Saturday
Collectable coins, Japanese swords,
Military relics. Estates, collections,
Accumulations, bought, sold and appraised.

LONDON
RANDY PLESTER ANTIQUES
Watch for new location.
519-434-4477 or 681-6349
We handle all types of antique
Furniture & collectibles.
Primitive, architectural, Victorian,
Depression, turn-of-the-century.

LONDON
HERITAGE SHOP ANTIQUES
357 Talbot Street   N6A 2R5
Just north of York Street
Tom Smits
519-439-9747
Open 10-4 daily, closed Sundays.
The very best in unique,
Fine & primitive antiques.

LONDON
THE ANTIQUARIAN
240 Richmond Street at Horton   N6B 2H6
519-432-4422
10-5 Tuesday thru Saturday.
Estate jewellery, pocket watches,
Sterling flatware, art glass,
Royal Doultons (many discontinued)
Fine old china, old prints, etc.
Please come in and browse!

LONDON
JEFFERSON STEREOPTICS
50 Foxborough Grove   N6K 4A8
John Saddy
519-641-4431
Stereo Card & Viewmaster.
International auctions.
Consignments accepted.
Consultations & evaluations.

LONDON
THE ANTIQUE COLLECTOR
1634 Hyde Park Road   N6H 5L7
Mr. Lynn Foley / Ms. Colleen Bogden
519-471-2499
9:30-5 Monday thru Saturday,
11-4 Sunday
Country pine & oak, primitives, sterling,
Victorian & Deco lighting, china, folk art,
Original paint, nostalgia, advertising.

LONDON
LONDON COIN & COLLECTABLES
345 Talbot Street   N6A 2R5
Deborah May, Bill Merkley
519-663-8099
Fax: 519-663-8019
9:30-5 Monday thru Friday,
9:30-4 Saturday.
Coins, paper money, stamps, china,
Glass, silver & jewellery.

LONDON
THE ANTIQUE EMPORIUM
765 Exeter Road, Unit #201   N6E 3T2
Just seconds north of Hwy. 401.
Kevin & Darlene Steele
519-668-8838
Fax: 519-668-6500
Website: www.antiqueemporium.on.ca
Open 7 days a week.
200 Individual antique
& Collectable showcases.

LONDON
THE ANTIQUITIES SHOPPE
129 Wellington at Hill   N6B 2K7
Bennett Grossman, Dan McLachlan
519-663-9400, 877-BENDAN1
E-mail: bendaninc@sprint.ca
Open 10-6 Monday thru Saturday,
12 Rooms of country Pine & oak.
Neon signs & decorator items,
Refinishing services available.
Internet consignment sales welcome.

MELBOURNE
HEXTER'S ANTIQUES
R.R. #1   N0L 1T0
Hwy. #2 west of London
Ted & Sheila Hexter
519-289-2170
By chance or please call.
China, glass,
Furniture and primitives.

PORT STANLEY
HARBOUR HOUSE
ANTIQUES AND UNIQUES
194 Main Street   N5L 1H6
Cliff Somerville
519-782-5108
Open seven days year round.
Furniture, china, glass, jewellery,
Collectibles, crafts, gifts, & art gallery.

ST. MARYS
R. O'HARA ANTIQUES
615 Queen Street East   N0M 2V0
R. O'Hara
519-284-3887
Open 8-5 daily.
Early furniture, glass, lamps.
Established over 40 years.

ST. MARYS – WOODHAM
THE ANTIQUITIES SHOPPE
WOODHAM HALL
5988 BaseLine Six, just east off Hwy. 23
10 mins. west of St. Marys   N0K 2A0
Bennett Grossman, Dan McLachlan
519-229-6600, 877-BENDAN 3
E-mail: bendaninc@sprint.ca
Strictly furniture, refinished and as found.
Hours, by chance (call ahead).
Internet consignment sales of collectables welcome.

SPARTA
ELIZABETH'S ANTIQUES
Main Street
Noon-5 Tuesday, Friday, Saturday & Sunday.
Early English Straffordshire, Flow Blue,
Canadian and American pressed glass,
Royal Copenhagen, Victoriana, silver,
Etchings and engravings, small furniture.
Objet d'art.

STRATFORD
ANTIQUES IN TIME
9 Market Place
Bruce Walsh, John Shantz
519-272-0411; Fax: 519-271-8336
E-mail: orc.ca./~time/
9:30-6 Monday thru Saturday.
Specializing in the sale and repair of
Antique clocks & watches.
In our 24th year of business.

STRATFORD
CAROL TELFER ANTIQUES
312 Cobourg Street   N5A 3G5
Carol Telfer
519-271-0941
By appointment & at shows.
Quilts, textiles, hooked rugs,
& Folk art.

STRATFORD
GREGORY CONNOR ANTIQUES
7 York Street   N5A 1A1
Across from the Court House.
519-273-4165
Open 10:30-2:30, Wednesday thru Friday,
11-4 Saturday & Sunday.
17th to early 19th century
Furnishings. Paintings,
Prints & porcelain.

STRATFORD
HIDDEN TREASURES ANTIQUES
432 Erie Street   N5A 2N5
Vernon & Marjorie Skinner
519-273-1940
Seven days a week, July & August.
Other months by chance or appointment.
Closed Christmas thru May 1st.
Antique furniture, glass,
China, books & collectables.

HERITAGE ANTIQUES

357 TALBOT STREET,
LONDON, ONTARIO
N6A 2R5
(519) 439-9747
TOM SMITS PROP.

City Centre Furniture

Antiques & Furniture

at Clarence & Horton, London

Phone: (519) 645-7533

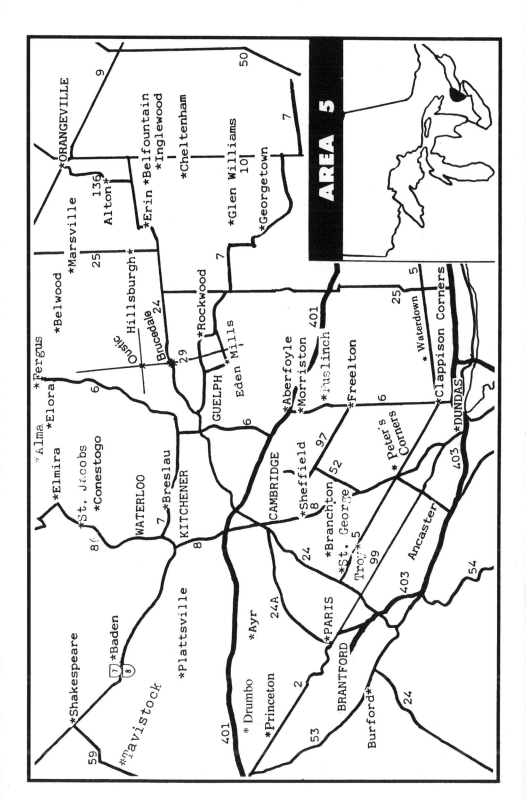

AREA 5

- 51 -

ABERFOYLE
ABERFOYLE ANTIQUE MARKET
Located south of Guelph,
Take Exit #299, off Hwy. 401,
Road #46 (Brock Road),
Go north 1.5 miles towards Guelph.
Open Sundays, 8-4.
April 30-October 29, 2000;
April 29-October 28, 2001.
519-763-1077
Adm. $1, kids free.

ABERFOYLE
BROCKHOUSE ANTIQUES
61 Brock Road   N1H 6H9
Next to Aberfoyle Antique Market
Paul Gillis
519-829-2966
10-5 Saturday and Sunday;
11-5 Monday and Friday.
Specializing in
Antique lighting and furniture.

ABERFOYLE
PARTNERS IN TYME
39 Brock Road south   N1H 6H9
Pauline Sinclair, Laura Anthony
519-827-1165
10-5 Wednesday thru Monday, closed Tuesday.
19th Century fine furniture, pine,
Interesting glass, china and silver.
Specializing in period pieces from the
1800s through to 1930s.

AYR
ANTIQUES AT THE SAWMILL
R.R. #1 Ayr (Roseville)   N0B 1E0
Bob & Edith Lenz
519-696-2911; 1-877 XMAS NUT
www.antiquesatthesawmill.com
10-4 Wednesday thru Friday,
12-6 Saturday & Sunday.
General line small antiques &
Furniture. Specializing in
Antique Christmas decorations.

BADEN
MEL'S ANTIQUES
13 Foundry Street   N0B 1G0
7 miles west of Kitchener off Hwy. 7 & 8.
Melvin Lee, 519-634-5088.
11-5 Tuesday thru Saturday,
Or by appointment.
Interesting selection of antiques,
Fine furnishings, pottery tools,
Primitives, clocks, glass & china.

BADEN
J.C. MILLER ANTIQUES
8 Foundry Street   N0B 1G0
519-634-8951
Canadian & American clocks,
Ontario country furnishings,
Quality kerosene lighting,
Glassware, china, folk art, &
Nostalgia.
Wholesaler – Retailer.

BRANTFORD
BROOKS' HOUSE ANTIQUES
248 Mt. Pleasant Street   N3T 1V1
Kathy & Ken Richards.
Open 7 days.
Full range of antiques &
Collectibles, memorabilia &
Nostalgia, Canadiana & Orientalia.
"Below market price."

BRANTFORD
GRIEVE'S MERCANTILE
14 Dalhousie Street   N3T 2H7
519-751-4333; 1-877-979-8285
June & Douglas Grieve
Tuesday thru Saturday 10-5;
Sunday 12-5; closed Monday.
Long and July/August weekends by chance
(Call ahead toll free).
Antiques, collectibles, advertising,
Toys & pre-1900s furniture.

CAMBRIDGE
SOUTHWORKS ANTIQUES MALL
64 Grand Avenue South   N1S 2L6
519-740-0110
Open 7 days (also by appointment after hours).
More than 30,000 sq. ft.
A fine selection of furniture, glassware,
Jewellery, nostalgia, and other collectibles.
Cafe on site featuring 1920s
Operational soda fountain.

CONESTOGA
ADELPHI ANTIQUES
23 King Street East   N0B 1N0
Lesley & Bob Bansen
519-664-1663
E-mail: lesleyb@nonline.net
1-5 Friday, 10-5 Saturday,
12-5 Sunday; or by appointment.
Antiques of distinction
& Collectibles.

CONESTOGA
ANTIQUES AND COLLECTABLES
43 King Street East   NOB 1N0
Bill & Marg McAllister
519-664-3088 (shop)
519-744-2083 (res.)
12-5 Saturday, Sunday & Holidays.
Monday thru Friday chance or appointment.
Furniture, china & nostalgia
Serving customers for over 20 years.

DRUMBO
HENRY DOBSON ANTIQUES LTD.
Box 216   N0J 1G0
Gibson Lane, off Oxford Road 29
Henry and Barbara Dobson
519-463-1147
By prior telephone arrangment.
English, Canadian and Continental
Period furniture and paintings.
Selected photos sent on request.

DUNDAS
ANOTHER TIME ANTIQUES at
DUNDAS VALLEY ANTIQUES
7 Main Street   L9H 2P7
Joyce Bravo
905-628-8876
10:30-4 Thursday,
10:30-4:30 Saturday & Sunday.
Victoriana, prints, linens.

DUNDAS
SALLY'S ANTIQUES at
DUNDAS VALLEY ANTIQUES
7 Main Street   L9H 2P7
Sally Lees
905-628-8876
10:30-4 Thursday,
10:30-4:30 Saturday & Sunday.
Furniture, glass, silver, etc.

DUNDAS
THE COLLECTIQUE SHOP at
DUNDAS VALLEY ANTIQUES
7 Main Street   L9H 2P7
Pegg & Gord Matthews
905-628-8876
10:30-4 Thursday,
10:30-4:30 Saturday & Sunday.
Furniture, china, lamps, etc.

DUNDAS
ZELDA'S COUNTRY LIVING ANTIQUES
at DUNDAS VALLEY ANTIQUES
7 Main Street   L9H 2P7
Rennie Geddes
905-628-8876
10:30-4 Thursday,
10:30-4:30 Saturday & Sunday.
Furniture, jewellery,
Art Deco, etc.

ELORA
THE ELORA ANTIQUE WAREHOUSE
6484 Wellington Road 7
Bill Little, P.O. Box 309   NOB 1S0
519-846-0305
Toll Free: 1-800-393-8715.
7 days, 10-6, all year.
15,000 sq. ft. & over 60 dealers.
Furniture, china & glass, books & art,
Pressed glass, nostalgia, collectibles.

ELORA - ALMA
PAUL NOONAN ANTIQUES
On Elora Road in Alma
4 miles north of Elora   NOB 1A0
519-846-9286
Open 10-5:30 Monday thru Saturday,
12:30-6 Sunday.
General line of antiques.
Dealers welcome.

FERGUS
KEN FEAKINS ANTIQUES &
FURNITURE REFINISHING
270 Bridge Street   N1M 1N5
Ken Feakins
519-843-1470
9:30 Monday thru Friday;
9-5 Saturday & Sunday.
Artwork, prints & oils, clocks, jewellery,
Lamps & primitives. Refinishing
Supplies, brass & wooden hardware.

FREELTON
FREELTON ANTIQUE MARKET
248 Freelton Road, P.O. Box 144 L0R 1K0
Fred &Char Berrisford
905-659-0948
Open year round
Thursday thru Sunday & Holiday Mondays.
120-Plus independent vendors.
Furniture, china, glass, collectibles,
Primitives, nostalgia.

SOUTHWORKS ANTIQUES

One of Canada's Largest Antique Malls

An Extensive Inventory of...

Furniture Primitive & Formal • Advertising • Pottery • Nostalgia
• Jewellery • Glass & China • Tins • Books • Bottles
• Silver • Toys and the unusual

And we offer...

• Quality Restoration, Refinishing and Upholstery Services:
SATISFACTION GUARANTEED
• Gift Certificates Available
• China Matching Service
• Layaway Plan • Searches for Wanted Items

Appraisal Service

Our appraisers have over 30 years experience in the "Antique Business."
They have also worked in conjunction with several museums and have conducted
many Private Estate and Insurance appraisals

Regular Hours
~ Open 7 Days

Mon.-Wed.   9:30 am - 6 pm • Thurs.-Fri.   9:30 am - 8 pm
Saturdays   9 am - 6 pm • Sundays   10 am - 6 pm
(*Other times by appointment*
• Call Doug or Laura Harding (519) 622-4517)

64 Grand Ave. South, Cambridge, Ontario, N1S 2L6
Tel.: (519) 740-0110 • Fax (519) 622-4517
Email: rustyb@golden.net

GUELPH
GALLERIES LA FINESSE OF GUELPH
"For those who appreciate the difference."
20 MacDonnell Street   N1H 2Z3
P.O. Box 1162
519-821-5850
Dorothy V. Hastings
Open 11-5:30, Tuesday thru Saturday.
Fine art, antiques, European imports,
Distinctive estate selections.

KITCHENER
ALAN'S ANTIQUES
681 Belmont Avenue West   N2M 1N3
Alan MacLeod
519-576-3311
10-5 Tuesday thru Friday;
9-10 Saturday, evenings by appointment.
Period and fine furniture,
Porcelains, china, crystal & silver.

KITCHENER
DUKE'S ANTIQUES INC.
386 Gage Avenue #1   N2M 5E1
Mary Ann Martin, Cathryn Finch.
Open 11-4:30 Monday thru Friday,
Saturday by chance. 519-743-1721.
Open by chance: July 15 thru August 15.
Summer hours: Suggest call ahead.
China, brass, glass, copper,
Jewellery & fine furniture.

KITCHENER
RUMNERS WOBBLE
720 Belmont Avenue   N2M 1P2
519-744-2932
Vernonica Wallner
Christina Wallner Rumble
10-5:30 Tuesday thru Thursday,
Friday 10-7, Saturday 10-5.
Antique furniture, mirrors,
Prints, china, glass, jewellery.

PARIS
STOCKS ANTIQUES
R.R. #2   N3L 3E2
519-442-7500 or 442-7007
Douglas Stocks
Open all year by appointment or
12-5 Saturday & Sunday.
Refinished pine, formal mahogany,
& Furniture in the rough
& Original finish.

PRINCETON
A PLACE IN TYME
16 Main Street North   N0J 1V0
519-458-4755
Winter: 7:30-7 Sunday thru Wednesday,
Summer: Open daily 7:30-9.
Antiques – Coffee House – General Store.
Operating as General Store since 1870.
Nostalgia, toys, dolls and other collectables.

ROCKWOOD
CASTLE'S ANTIQUES
Corner #7 Highway & Main Street
111 Main St., P.O. Box 848   N0B 2K0
519-856-0188; 888-363-0662
Phil & Darlene Castle
10-6 Tuesday thru Sunday.
Country furniture and accessories,
Refinished by hand or in
Original painted condition.

ST. GEORGE
BABES IN THE WOODS ANTIQUES
General Delivery   N0E 1N0
Peter & Lorene Hildrop
519-448-9992
Show dealers, also exhibiting at
Southworks, Cambridge and Classic Vault,
St. George.
General line of quality glass, china, silver.
Specializing in fine lace, linens, old dolls,
Carriages, etc.

ST. GEORGE
CLASSIC VAULT EMPORIUM
12 Main Street, P.O. Box 231 N0E 1N0
519-448-1483
Jean Hastings and
Kate's Korner's of Ed's Antiques
Jan.-Mar. 11-5, Tuesday thru Sunday,
Apr.-Dec. 10-5 Seven days.
Antiques and collectibles,
Old books.

ST. GEORGE
SHIRLEY'S ANTIQUES & COLLECTIBLES
2 and 6 Main Street   N0E 1N0
519-448-1861; Fax: 519-751-7150
Shirley Swift
11-5 Tuesday thru Sunday
Specializing in Victorian –
Formal and country furniture and
Accessories.
Articles bought and sold.

ST. GEORGE
THE MACS ANTIQUES
R.R. #1   N0E 1N0
(Watch for sign at Hwy. 5 & Sager Rd.)
Patricia & Clarence McIntyre
519-448-1655
Open 2-5 daily, other times
By chance or appointment.
Offering one of the largest selections of
Antiques & collectibles in the province.

ST. JACOBS
ST. JACOBS ANTIQUE MARKET
The Old Factory, 8 Spring Street   N0B 2N0
Ron Hook
519-664-1243; Fax: 519-664-3079.
www.antiquemall.on.ca
10-6 Monday thru Saturday;
12:30-5:30 Sunday.
Multi-dealer shop.
Eclectic range of antiques, nostalgia,
Collectibles, fun & unusual items.

ST. JACOBS
THE WATERLOO COUNTY ANTIQUE WAREHOUSE
805 King St. North/Regional Rd. 15   N0B 2N0
Next to the Farmers Market
519-725-2644, Toll Free: 1-888-843-9929
7 Days, 10-6 all year.
15,000 Sq. ft. and over 80 dealers.
Furniture, china & glass, books & art,
Pressed glass, nostalgia, collectibles.

SHAKESPEARE
GLEN MANOR GALLERIES
19 & 21 Huron Road West   N0B 2P0
Brian P. Campbell, Carl J. Booth
519-625-8920
Open daily year round.
Antiques & formal furniture,
Moorecroft & art pottery,
Art glass & 19th century china.

SHAKESPEARE
JONNY'S ANTIQUES LTD.
Corner Hwys. #7 & 8, and Hwy. #59   N0B 2P0
519-625-8307
Open 10-6 Monday thru Saturday,
11-6 Sunday.
18th, 19th & early 20th Century
Porcelain & glass.
Formal & country furniture,
Art Nouveau & Art Deco.

SHAKESPEARE
LAND & ROSS ANTIQUES
29 Huron Road, 2 Fraser Street   N0B 2P0
519-625-8070
Open daily year round.
Specializing in Canadian
Antique furniture.
Custom reproduction furniture
And accessories.

TAVISTOCK
THE GLASS SWAN
52 Woodstock Street South
P.O. Box 659   N0B 2R0
Bill & Jean Swanink
519-655-2041
Open seven days.
Antiques, primitives, nostalgia,
Custom stained glass.

Promoters

 Don't Forget to Advertise your shows!

~ *Notes* ~

ANTIQUES IN HAMLET

JONNY'S ANTIQUES

●

(519) 625-8307

●

Formal and country furniture,
researched and identified
18th, 19th and early 20th century
porcelain and glass.
Member of the Canadian
Antique Dealers Association.

LAND & ROSS ANTIQUES

●

29 Huron Road West
and 2 Fraser Street

(519) 625-8070

●

Specializing in Canadian
Antique Furniture,
Custom Reproduction Furniture
and Accessories.

Just a few minutes east of Stratford,
and perfect for a lazy Sunday afternoon's drive,
you can enjoy the charm and pleasures of Shakespeare

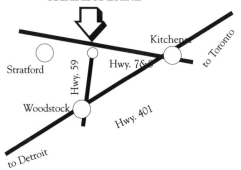

since 1959

CANADA'S OLDEST and LARGEST
OUTDOOR ANTIQUE MARKET
~ Celebrating 41 Years ~

Aberfoyle Antique Market

Furniture • Memorabilia • Jewelry • Collectibles

Over 100
Antique
Dealers,
kids play area,
a restaurant,
and plenty
of clean,
fresh country air

$1 Admission
KIDS FREE
(12 & under)

☎ **(519) 763-1077**
OPEN SUNDAYS 8-4
APRIL 30 - OCT. 29, 2000

"Located south
of Guelph.
Take Hwy. #401 to Exit
#299, Road #46 (Brock
Rd).
Go north towards
Guelph 1-1/2 miles to
Aberfoyle."

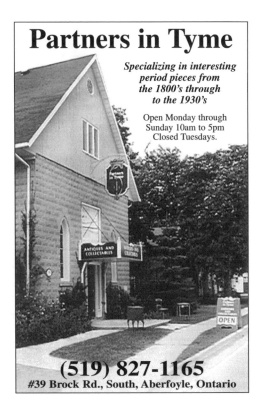

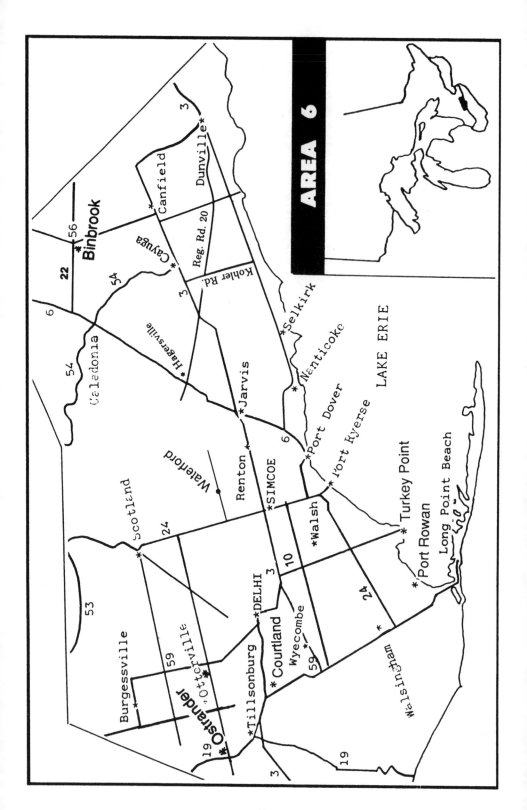

AREA 6

LAKE ERIE

Binbrook
Canfield
Dunville
Cayuga
Reg. Rd. 20
Kohler Rd.
Selkirk
Nanticoke
Hagersville
Caledonia
Jarvis
Port Dover
Port Ryerse
Renton
Waterford
SIMCOE
Walsh
Turkey Point
Scotland
Port Rowan
Long Point Beach
DELHI
Courtland
Wyecombe
Burgessville
Otterville
Tillsonburg
Ostrander
Walsingham

BINBROOK
DUVALL'S ANTIQUES
And Old Furniture
2471 Guyatt Road East, R.R. #1   L0R 1C0
905-692-3333
10-5, Seven days.
Th&B memorabilia, radios
Canadian & imported furniture,
Glass, china, brass,
Frames, etc.

CAYUGA
QUEST END ANTIQUES & WHATNOTS
R.R. #2   N0A 1E0
Jim & Wilma Louks
905-774-3991
At shows or by appointment.
Glass, oil lamps, tools, primitives,
Grain scales & furniture.
Also at Memory Lane at Hyde Park, London.

DELHI
ANTIQUE MARKET
107 Main Street,
Mailing: Box 129, Langton   N0E 1G0
Pat Poole
519-428-5743 Bus.; 519-875-2465 Res.
10-5 Tuesday thru Sunday, closed Monday.
Thirteen dealer co-op.
Wide range of collectibles, furniture, glass,
Advertising, toys and nostalgia, etc.

OSTRANDER
OSTRANDER ANTIQUES
THE ANTIQUE HOUSE
COBWEBS & CANDLESTICKS
THE DEACON'S BENCH
On Hwy. 19, north of Tillsonburg.
519-842-4444 – Les & Helen Vanka
10-4:30 Wednesday thru Saturday.
Furniture, collectables, pottery,
Glass, china & quilts, etc.

PORT DOVER
21ST ANNUAL ANTIQUE SHOW & SALE
Port Dover Lion's Club
at the Community Centre
Info: 519-583-2740
Saturday, September 30th, 2000, 10-6;
Sunday, October 1st, 2000, 10-5.
30 Selected dealers.
Free parking,
Admission $3, light lunches available.

PORT DOVER
22nd ANNUAL ANTIQUE SHOW & SALE
Port Dover Lion's Club
at the Community Centre
Info: 519-583-2740
Saturday, September 29th, 2001, 10-6
Sunday, September 30th, 2001, 10-5
30 Selected dealers, free parking
Admission $3, light lunches available.

SELKIRK
MILLER'S CURIOSITY SHOP
Main Street   N0A 1P0
Bill & Joyce Miller
416-776-2838
Open 10-5 Seven days/week.
Country furniture, accessories, china,
Glass, repro. brass hardware, custom
Refinishing. Additional warehouse –
5,000 Sq. ft. Furniture in the rough.

SIMCOE
COUNTRY CORNER ANTIQUES
R.R. #1 Simcoe   N3Y 4J9
5 Miles west on Hwy. #3
Frank & Frances Feth
519-426-8240
Open 11-5 Seven days/week,
Or by appointment.
Pine & oak furniture, pottery, primitives,
Glass & china. We buy & sell.

SIMCOE
ROOT CELLAR ANTIQUES
R.R. #2
75 Lynn Valley Road   N3Y 4K1
Jerry & Leona Milne
519-428-4633
By chance or appointment, please call ahead.
Early Canadiana, refinished
Furniture & related accessories.

WATERFORD
C.J.'s ANTIQUES & REFINISHING
R.R. #4 on Hwy. #24,
8 miles north of Simcoe   N0E 1Y0
Keith & Diane Koopman
519-443-4197 or 443-5853
Open 8:30-4 Monday thru Saturday,
12:30-4 Sunday.
Largest antique furniture shop in Ontario.
Come & see our showroom.

WATERFORD
TOWNSEND'S TREASURES
St. James Street South
Don & Jane Townsend
519-443-7044
10-5 daily.
Pharmaceutical items,
Furniture, china and glass.

WYECOMBE - DELHI
O.C. TRADING
In the village of Wyecombe
County Rd. #21, 2 miles east of Langton
R.R. #1 Delhi   N4B 2W4
519-875-4972
Quality Canadian country furniture,
In the rough or refinished.
Textiles & accessories.
Selection of folk art.

~ Notes ~

PARTIAL LIST OF
AMERICAN CUT GLASS MANUFACTURERS

Baltimore Bargain House
Baltimore, Maryland
1890
Baltimore Bargain House

George Borgfeldt & Co.
New York, N.Y.
1912

 Corning Glass Works
Corning, N.Y.
1904

C. Dorflinger & Sons
White Mills, Pa.
1892

 O.F. Eggington
Corning, N.Y.
1890

 T.G. Hawkes
Corning, N.Y.
1890

Lotus Cut Glass Co.
Barnesville, Ohio
1898

 Pairpoint Corp.
New Bedford, Mass.
1898

 J.D. Bergen
Meriden, Conn.
1894

T.B. Clarke & Co.
Seelyville, Pa.
1898

 Corona Cut Glass Co.
Toledo, Ohio
1906

Thomas Drysdale & Co.
New York, N.Y.
1886

 H.C. Fry Glass Co.
Toledo, Ohio
1895

 Libbey Glass Co.
Toledo, Ohio
1895

Mount Washington Glass Co.
South Boston, Mass.
1892

L. Straus & Sons
New York, N.Y.
1894

PARTIAL LIST OF
CANADIAN CUT GLASS MANUFACTURERS

Belleville Cut Glass Co.
Belleville, Ont.
1912
unmarked

Gowans, Kent & Co.
Toronto, Ont.
1905
ELITE

Lakefield Cut Glass Co.
Lakefield, Ont.
1915
Sometimes a small Union Jack

George Phillips & Co., Ltd.
Montreal, Que.
1907
not known

Henry Birks & Sons
Montreal, Que.
1904   **BIRKS**

 Gundy-Clapperton
Montreal, Que.
1905

Ottawa Cut Glass Co.
Ottawa, Ont.
1913
not known

Roden Brothers
Toronto, Ont.
1910

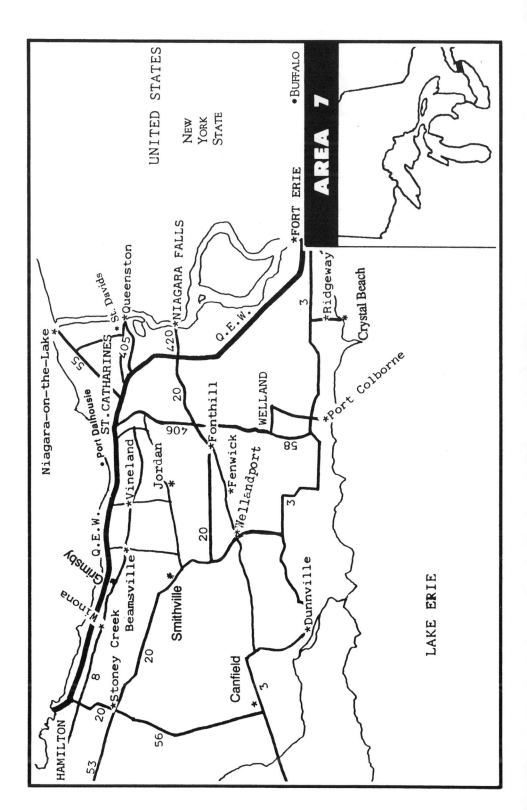

KELLY & KORMOS

queenston antiques

93 QUEENSTON STREET

Historical Queenston Village
(across from the school)
Phone (905) 262-4796

Historical Queenston Village is situated on the Niagara River between Niagara Falls and Niagara-on-the-Lake, across from Lewiston, New York, three minutes fron the Queenston-Lewiston Bridge, 10 minutes from the Queen Elizabeth Way.

Ont. Cherry Tall Post Bed c/w Tester, circa 1830

We Offer:

... Quality pre-confederation formal and country furniture and accessories in an 1807 setting: -including
... Tiger, birds eye and flame pieces.
... Rare Niagara Peninsula pieces.
... The largest selection of early beds and tall four posters in Canada. Beds in singles, 3/4's, doubles, queens, and kings, even pairs.
BEDS - maple, birch, cherry, etc. finish & original paint.
BEDS - Low-post, cannonball, bell, acorn, tulip, pineapple; also rope-twist & carved.
BEDS - Sleigh, half-tester, plantation, high Victorian & Edwardian.

BUYING & SELLING

WITH INTEGRITY

Your Personal Invitation to Visit

GRANNY'S BOOT ANTIQUES

For Unique Finds in Antiques & Country Pine

Our stock is contantly changing. We offer Quality, Quantity and most of all - Fair Prices.

Some pieces are very rare. Many are oddities that even the experts are stumped on. Others are very primitive - stretching the imagination - and still others are quite the norm.

Designers and Decoratotrs alike will find everything for their decorating needes. A real Tresure Hunt for Collectors.

GRANNY'S BOOT
ANTIQUES & COUNTRY PINE
Prop.: Madge L. Wilson

**Hours: Tues. - Sun. 11-5
Closed Mon. - except holidays.**

3389 King St., Vineland
(905) 562-7055
www.grannysbootantiques.com
e-mail: infor.@grannysbootantiques.com

WHEN
Visiting
Antique Shops
Mention

Antique
Showcase
Directory

Dealers appreciate knowing where their advertising is being see.

BEAMSVILLE
WALKER HALL TEA ROOM & ANTIQUES
4927 30 Road North   L0R 1B3
Dale & Richard Torch
905-563-5204
10-3 Mon.-Thurs., 11-5 Sat. & Sun.
Step back in time, majestic estate
Home on Lake Ontario. Delicious
Homemade luncheons. Unique experience,
& Selection of antiques & collectibles.

CRYSTAL BEACH
ANTIQUE ANNIE
34 Queen Circle   L0S 1B0
Ann Bower – 16th Season
905-894-4951
12-5 Saturday, Sunday & Holidays.
May thru Sept., or phone ahead.
Antiques & collectibles – lace, linens, quilts,
Vintage clothing, bottles, flatware.
Dealers welcome.

CRYSTAL BEACH
BLACKBEARD'S TREASURE AUCTION
377 Derby Road, P.O. Box 853   L0S 1B0
R. Blackbeard Snr. Auctions/Sales
905-894-2984
By chance or appointment.
Estates, liquidations, bankruptcies,
House & farm sales. Also specializing in fine
Persian carpets, antique & new. Large showroom.

FONTHILL
EFFINGHAM HILLS ANTIQUES
(2 locations)
135 Hwy. 20 East, 905-892-0412
Paul & Betty Samuel
10-5:30 Open 7 days.
1619 Effingham Street, 905-892-9861
10-4 Wed. thru Sund., closed Mon. & Tues.
E-mail: effinghamhills@hotmail.com
Website: www.vaxxine.com/effinghamhills
Late 19th - early 20th century
Furniture & accessories.

FONTHILL
TREASURE TROVE
The Trading Post on Hwy. #20
Jean & Jack Gray
905-892-4340 or 892-3638 (res.)
Open seven days.
Victorian furniture, china,
Art glass.
Also at Jordan Antique Centre.

HAMILTON
LOCKE STREET ANTIQUES
200 Locke Street South   L8P 4B4
905-526-6553
10:30-5:30 Tues., Wed. & Thurs.,
10:30-7:30 Fri., 10-5:30 Sat., closed Sun.
Good selection of antiques &
Collectibles, furniture, etc.

HAMILTON
THREE SMALL ROOMS
Marion G. Hetherington
905-525-3544
By appointment only or at shows.
Collectors' calls are welcome.
Quality antiques including
Victoriana & Orientals.

HAMILTON - STONEY CREEK
EXCELLENT FURNITURE REPAIRS
407 Hwy. 20 South
P.O. Box #9, Stoney Creek   L8G 3X4
John Checchia
905-561-8560 or 561-2727
Open seven days.
If coming a distance, please phone first.
Antiques & fine furniture, restoration &
Refinishing. Will sell on consignment.

JORDAN
BRITTANIC ANTIQUES
3836 Main Street   L0R 1S0
Tony & Margaret Cliff
905-562-7944
Open daily 10 a.m. - 5 p.m.
Closed Monday, January - April.
4,000 Square feet showroom – A selective
Collection of antiques & decorative items.
Dining & bedroom suites.

JORDAN
BROWSERS MARKET
3744 Main Street   L0R 1S0
Tom or Joyce
905-562-7613
11-5 Wednesday thru Sunday,
Or by appointment.
Antiques and collectables, including
Toys, garden furniture, tools.
Always the unusual.

JORDAN
MRS. AUDREY E. GRIFFITH
3804 Main Street   L0R 1S0
off Hwy. 81 – near Jordan Museum
905-562-4666
Open every day, but phoning
Ahead is advisable.
Canadian and American pattern glass,
China, silver, books, oils and watercolours
By well known artists. Over 42 years in business.

JORDAN
J. HAGERAATS ANTIQUE LIGHTING
3837 Main Street   L0R 1S0
James hageraats
905-562-7441
10-5, Wednesday thru Sunday
Antique lighting,
Furniture and gifts.

JORDAN
JORDAN ANTIQUES CENTRE
3836 Main Street   L0R 1S0
Tony & Margaret Cliff
905-562-7723
Open daily 10 a.m. - 5 p.m.
Closed Monday, January - April.
7,000 Square feet of variety –
Furniture, China, glass,
Lighting, linens and toys.

JORDAN
JORDAN VILLAGE ANTIQUES
ALLEN TIFFANEY ANTIQUES
19th Street – Across from the Firehall
1/4 Mile north of Regional Rd. 81 (Hwy. 8)
905-322-1194
10-5 Friday, Saturday, Sunday,
Or by appointment or chance.
Look for extended summer hours.
Antiques & collectibles – multi dealer shop.

JORDAN
PARKWOOD GALLERIES
3845 Main Street   L0R 1S0
905-562-5415
1-877-337-4577
Website: www.parkwoodgalleries.com
10-5 Daily
Closed Mondays in January.
Specializing in fine furnishings,
Decorative arts & collectibles.

NIAGARA-ON-THE-LAKE
ANTIQUES AT THE ICE CREAMERY
758 Niagara Stone Road, Hwy. #55
905-641-0861   L0S 1J0
Open daily at 11 a.m., seven days.
Multi-dealer summer market
May 1st thru October 31st, each year.
Exquisite antiques to uniques
And cool old stuff.

NIAGARA-ON-THE-LAKE
LAKESHORE ANTIQUES & TREASURES
855 Lakeshore Road, RR #3   L0S 1J0
905-646-1965
10-5, every day, year round
Multi-dealer co-op.
On Niagara's scenic wine route.
We offer pre-Victorian to Retro,
Country to nostalgia.

NIAGARA-ON-THE-LAKE (VIRGIL)
NIAGARA STONE ROAD ANTIQUES
1516 Niagara Stone Road,
P.O. Box 322, Virgil   L0S 1T0
905-468-1795
Louise Lidstone
11-5 Wednesday thru Sunday.
Antiques and collectibles.
China, glass, small furniture & accessories.
'Anything that can be handled by one person.'

NIAGARA-ON-THE-LAKE
NOTHING NEW ANTIQUES
1823 Niagara Stone Road, Hwy. #55
905-468-7016
Ginny Dyck
Summer: open seven days, 10:30-5
Spring & fall: Friday thru Sunday only.
Winter: Saturday & Sunday, or by appointment.
Country & Victorian furniture,
Glassware, quilts, china, etc.

NIAGARA-ON-THE-LAKE
RED BARN ANTIQUE MALL
2017 Niagara Stone Road   L0S 1J0
R.R. #3, Hwy. #55, 2 min's from N-O-T-L.
Tel./Fax: 905-468-0900.
10-6, every day, year round,
Closed Christmas & New Year's day.
Large selection of reasonably
Priced quality antiques.
From over 35 dealers.

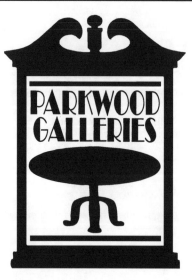

ST. DAVID'S
ANNA'S ANTIQUES & COLLECTIBLES
253 Creek Road   L0S 1P0
Anna & Edge Futino
905-262-5524; 905-356-0823 (after hours)
11-5 Summer, seven days,
Off-season, Wednesday thru Sunday.
Furniture, china, glass
& Collectibles.

ST. DAVID'S
S&B ANTIQUES
246 Creek Road (P.O. Box 249)   L0S 1P0
Shirley & Bruce Shevel
905-262-2007
E-mail: shevel@caninet.com
Website: http://www.caninet.com/~sbantiq
11-5 Seven days,
Closed Monday & Tuesday, January-March.
Furniture, glass, china,
Oil lamps, and collectibles.

VINELAND
GRANNY'S BOOT ANTIQUES
3389 King Street (formerly Main Street)
Box 564   L0R 2C0
Madge L. Wilson; 905-562-7055
E-mail: info.@grannysbootantiques.com
Website: www.grannysbootantiques.com
Open 11-5 Tuesday thru Sunday.
Primitives, folk art, unique works of art.
Custom designed antiques of the future.
Prop rentals & finders service.

VINELAND
PRUDHOMMES ANTIQUE MARKET
Prudhommes Landing North Service Road
Exit 55 or 57, off QEW
905-562-5187
105- Firday, Saturday, Sunday all year.
Multi-dealer antique market.
Antiques and collectibles,
Furniture, glass, china,
Vintage clothing and linens.

VINELAND
R.J.'S ANTIQUES & THINGS
3831 Victoria Avenue South, Box 159   L0R 2C0
Just 1/2 km. south of Hwy. 8
Ron & Carol Thompson
905-562-3933
11-5 Friday thru Saturday,
10-5 Sunday & Holiday Mondays,
Other times by chance.
A wide selection of antiques,
Collectibles, nostalgia & memorabilia.

Chairs Through the Ages

Chairs: mid and late Georgian. first row: 1770s-90s. Oval back, curved legs; vase-shaped (shield) back, serpentine seat, tapering legs; squarer style of the 1790s with its splat in urn outline; upholstered bergère. Second row: two examples of the 1790s; two of the 1800s, one with a caned seat, the other dipped.

Regional and country chairs. First row: 17th century. Folding, so-called Glastonbury, early; two so-called Yorkshire-Derbyshire types, the seats sunk for cushions, mid-century; back of Carolean armchair with flat splats shaped to resemble twist turning. Second row: 18th century. Country modification of Queen Anne curved-back cabriole-legged single chair; country ladder back and spindle back, with rush seats and prominent front stretchers, with alternative back designs.

Regional and country chairs. First row: Windsor types. Two early comb-backs; the hoop-back at its simplest with central splat; detail of a typical late "wheel" splat; plan hoop-back with saddle seat and stretchers to the cabriole legs. Second row: ornate splat hoop-back with hooped "crinoline" front stretcher; late so-called Lancashire Windsor, heavy turned supports; child's, movable footboard; so-called Suffolk version.

A SOCIABLE DISEASE

The doctor's head shook sadly
"There isn't any cure.
You're suffering an ailment
of origin obscure.

It's known as "Antiquitis"
And once it has a hold…
There's nothing anyone can do
To help you, so I'm told.

There'll be some disillusion,
Of which you are aware…
Then pangs of disappointment
Turn to hours of dark despair;

And there'll be other, happy days,
When right out of the blue
Will fall the greatest treasure
That has ever come to you.

Mile on mile you'll travel
Til your mind and legs are weak,
Looking, browsing, searching for
The nostalgic and unique…

As your doctor, I'm concerned
That you are well and sound;
"Antiquitis" is contagious, and
There's much of it around.

Here's my telephone number,
I'd appreciate it if you would
Call me at any hour…
If you come on something good."

By Shirley G. Cole

Pair of 19th century Naval Cannon. Overall length 7ft. 6 in.

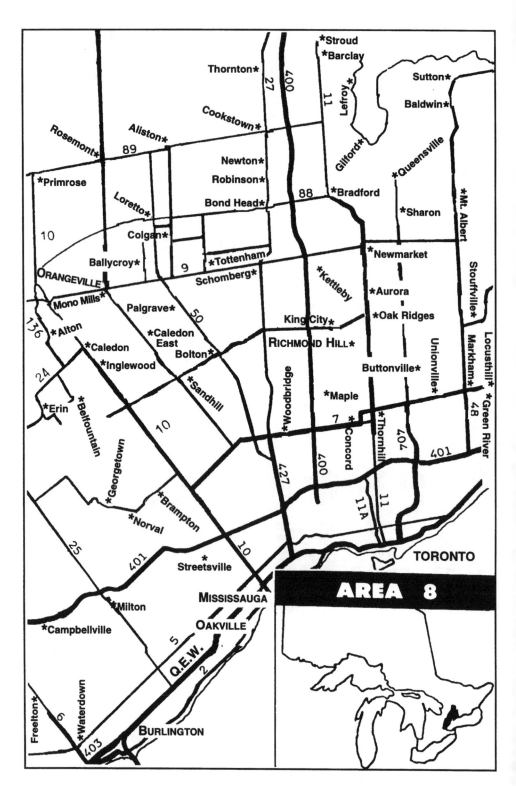

BOND HEAD
MUDD FLOORS ANTIQUES
N.E. corner of Hwy. 88 & Hwy. 27
4334 Hwy. 88, P.O. Box 208   L0G 1B0
905-778-0376
Marks Sand, Michael Ibbott.
Open most days.
By chance or appointment.
Misson, early Canadian and
Decorative finds.

BOND HEAD
ROSE HILL INTERIORS & ANTIQUES
N.W. corner of Hwy. 27 & 5th Line
R.R. 1, Stn. Main, Bradford   L3Z 2A4
905-939-2244; Fax: 905-939-2243
9-5 Saturday, Sunday & Holidays
Friday p.m. or by appointment.
Antiques and collectables. Canadiana,
Victorian furniture and accessories.
Century wood reconstructed furnishings.

BRAMPTON
CANADIAN DEPRESSION GLASS ASSN.
Established in 1976
119 Wexford Road   L6Z 2T5
905-846-2835
Membership: 1 yr. $15, 3 yrs. $40.
Newsletter: 6/year includes: D.G. topics,
Dealer Directory, advts., reproduction
Alerts, show reports, etc.
Preservationists of Depression era glassware.

BRAMPTON
TIMES GONE BY
45 Queen Street East   L6W 2A7
One block east of Main Street
Voweth Van Gent
905-455-7545
Varied selection of
Antiques & collectibles.
Buy – Sell – Consignment

BRAMPTON
WALTZ TIME ANTIQUES
119 Wexford Road   L6Z 2T5
Walter Lemiski
905-846-2835
E-mail: wlemiski@home.com
Full range of Depression glass
Mail order
Or by appointment.

BURLINGTON
TOWNLINE ANTIQUES
905-335-5488
Barb & Ray Long
Georgian, Victorian
Edwardian jewellery,
China, perfumes,
Boxes & art glass.
Exhibiting at show sales and
Jordan Antique Centres.

BURLINGTON
TYPICAL COLLECTOR ANTIQUES
Upper Brant
P.O. Box 40524   L7P 4W1
905-335-0511
Antique Show Exibitors.
Victorian Cranberry glass,
Early porcelains,
Art glass & perfurmes.

CALEDON
INGLEWOOD ANTIQUE MARKET
16083 Hwy. #10 Hurontario St.   L0N 1C0
15 minutes north of Brampton
Annette & Phil Turturia
905-838-4000
E-mail: annephil@idirect.com
Open year round.
Great variety of everything.
From country to traditional.

CALEDON
RAINBARREL ANTIQUES
17 George Street   L0N 1C0
Shirley Campbell
519-927-1797
10-5 Tuesday thru Saturday, 11-5 Sunday.
Hand-finished country furniture, farm tools,
Primitives and accessories. Repro hardware.
Barn full "in the rough". (By appointment).

CALEDON
WOODEN BUCKET ANTIQUES
Hwy. 10 & 24
Jean Lynch
519-927-3560
Selected pieces of
Canadiana & accessories.

37th ANNUAL

MARKHAM ANTIQUE SHOW

SEPTEMBER 15, 16, 17, 2000

MOUNT JOY COMMUNITY CENTRE
HWY. 48 & 16TH AVENUE

FRIDAY	5:00 p.m. - 9:30 p.m.
SATURDAY	10:00 a.m. - 6:00 p.m.
SUNDAY	11:00 a.m. - 5:00 p.m.

ADMISSION $4.00 per day
14 and under free with an adult

• OVER 40 DEALERS • HOURLY DOOR PRIZES
• REFRESHMENTS AVAILABLE

SPONSORED BY
MARKHAM LIONS CLUB

FOR INFOMATION CONTACT
Lion Mike Hiatt
905-294-1510

CAMPBELLVILLE
MARNALEA ANTIQUES
51 Main Street North, Box 152   LOP 1B0
905-854-0287; Fax: 905-854-3117
E-mail: doulton@marnalea.com
Bill Krever
Open weekends or by chance or appointment.
Discontinued Royal Doulton
Figurines & jugs,
Worcester & Paragon figurines.

CAMPBELLVILLE
REGENCY HOUSE ANTIQUES
87 Main Street North, "Guelph Line"
Box 159   LOP 1B0
905-854-2727
A multi-dealer complex.
Jan. 1 thru Apr. 30: Fr. thru Mon. 11-5,
May 1 thru Dec. 31: seven days, 11-5.
Fine formal & country furniture, china,
Oil lamps, glass, prints, clocks & Canadiana.

CAMPBELLVILLE
THE STONE HOUSE OF CAMPBELLVILLE
Guelph Line, 1/2 mile south
of Campbellville
P.O. Box 137   LOP 1B0
The Singletons 905-854-2152
E-mail: the-stonehouse@yahoo.com
Open 9-5, seven days.
Imported stained glass windows,
Mainly from England.

COOKSTOWN
COOKSTOWN ANTIQUE & ART CENTRE
10 Queen Street South   L0L 1L0
705-458-0903
Open daily.
Quality and variety in antiques
& Collectibles.
Jewellery, flatware, art, militaria,
Porcelain, glass, period & country furniture.

COOKSTOWN
COOKSTOWN ANTIQUE MARKET
Hwy. 27 1 km. north of Hwy. 89
Beside school, 5 minutes from Hwy. 400
Sally & Gerry Robinson
705-458-1275, Fax: 458-1847
Open 7 days.
Furniture, china, glass, jewellery,
Nostalgia, primitives, linens, lace.
Displayed by 40 dealers.

COOKSTOWN
COOKSTOWN CASTLE ANTIQUES CENTRE
7 King Street North   L0L 1L0
NE corner of Main Intersection.
705-458-0836. Open seven days 10-5.
22 vendor displays of quality antiques
& Collectibles, in a medieval atmosphere.
Your home is your Castle.
Our treasures await you...
Plenty of parking available.

COOKSTOWN
ROADSHOW ANTIQUES
N.E. corner of Hwy. 400
at Hwy. 89 (Cookstown exit)
65 Reive Blvd., P.O. Box 29   L0L 1L0
705-458-9898 Fax 705-458-8998
Summer: 10-6 Mon. thru Fri., 9-6 Sat. & Sun.
Winter: 11-6 Mon. thru Fri., 9-6 Sat. & Sun.
30,000 Square feet of quality antiques
Fine art, collectibles, memorabilia.

COOKSTOWN
RUS IN URBE HABERDASHERY
9 Queen Street, P.O. Box 384   L0L 1L0
705-458-1387
Wreford G. Nix, B.A.
Antiques & collectibles.
Multi-dealer mall.
Open daily year round plus
Tea room and
Fashion & Gift Boutique.

COOKSTOWN
THE COUNTRY IMAGE
23 Queen Street, P.O. Box 388   L0L 1L0
705-458-4850
Jeff Spence
Tuesday thru Sunday (Monday by chance)
Antique furniture, fine china,
Fine furnishings, old wicker
& Giftware
We buy & sell any items of interest.

COOKSTOWN
WILL SILK'S GENERAL STORE
14 Queen Street, P.O. Box 232   L0L 1L0
705-458-9212
Laurie & Glen Munroe
10-5 Monday thru Saturday, 11-5 Sunday
Antiques & collectibles,
Cornflower Crystal, Wades,
Coke memorabilia, die-cast,
Fudge, candy, gourment foods.

INGLEWOOD ANTIQUE MARKET

TM

16083 Hurontario St.,
Caledon, Ontario
On east side of Hwy #10 2km
south of Forks of Credit Rd.

- *Formal Furniture*
- *Primitive Pine*
- *Glass & China*
- *Vintage Lighting*

- *Architectural Antiques*
- *Quilts & Linens*
- *Jewellery & Silver*
- *Decorating Accents*

OPEN YEAR ROUND
905-838-4000
e-mail: annephil@idirect.com

GREEN RIVER – LOCUST HILL
MICHAEL ROWAN ANTIQUES
R.R. #1 Locust Hill   L0H 1J0
Corner of Hwy. 7 & Side Road
#34 Green River
Michael Rowan
416-471-5511
By chance or appointment
Folk art, paintings, antique furniture.
Wholesale, appraisals.

GREENWOOD
POLLIKERS
2370 Concessin 6   L0H 1H0
Gerry Marks
905-427-4498
Hours vary – appointment suggested.
Early pine furniture,
Painted or refinished.
Primitives & folk art.

LOCUST HILL
PAST REFLECTION ANTIQUES
7861 Hwy. 7 (3 miles east of Markham Rd.)
Helen Van Rooy and Robert Irwin
905-472-9891 or 905-649-3325 (res.)
Fax: 905-649-5232
11-5 Friday, 10-5 Saturday, Sunday & Holidays
Selection of oak, walnut, mahogany and
Pine furniture and accessories, displayed in
Two extensive ca. 1860 Heritage buildings.

MARKHAM
37TH ANNUAL ANTIQUE SHOW & SALE
Mount Joy Community Centre
Hwy. 48 & 16th Ave., behind Sunkist Market.
Fri., Sept. 15 – 5-9:30; Sat.,
Sept. 16 – 10-6; Sun., Sept. 17 – 11-5.
Admission $4.00.
Sponsored by Markham Lions Club.
Mike Hiatt, Chairman 2000
905-294-1510.

MARKHAM
FITZHENRY & WHITESIDE
195 Allstate Parkway   L3R 4T8
905-477-9700
8:30-4:30 Monday thru Friday.
Distributors of Unitt's Price Guides
And other related antique publications.
Direct order line:
905-477-2659 or 2499.

MARKHAM
G&P ANTIQUES
91 Anderson Avenue #4   L6E 1A5
Paolo Biasutti
905-471-6023
8-6 Monday thru Friday,
Saturday & Sunday by appointment.
Specializing in refinishing &
Restoration of antiques.
Custom woodworking.

MARKHAM
McCOWAN ANTIQUES & REFINISHING
10690 McCowan Road   L3P 3J3
Gerard Van Dyk
905-640-8442
www.canadiana-antiques.com.
Open seven days..
Antiques & refinishing.
Restoration and repairs.

MILTON
C and J ENTERPRISES
AUCTIONEERS
1229 Marlborough Crt., #803
Oakville   L6H 3B6
Joan Cooke, C. Frank Hall
905-338-0681
Full auction services.
Single items – complete estates.

MISSISSAUGA
DUNCAN ROBERT ANTIQUES
1740 Saltdene Terrace   L4W 2E4
Boyd Suttie
416-625-8984
Appointment arrangement anytime.
Antique scientific instruments:
Brass microscopes, medical,
Dental & laboratory items.
Navigational, surveying items.

MISSISSAUGA
MARCELLE ANTIQUES
Mirko & Marcelle Melis
905-689-1648
Exhibiting at major shows
Or by appointment only.
American & European art glass,
Fine English & continental porcelains,
Victorian to Art Deco jewellery.

MISSISSAUGA
PAUL'S ANTIQUES
3045 Southcreek Rd., Unit 45   L4X 2X7
905-629-0992
Paul & Celeste Demelo
Specializing in turn-of-the-century
Mahogany furniture.
Dining & bedroom suites
& Occasional pieces.

MISSISSAUGA
THE BARN
1675 Lakeshore Road West   L5J 1J4
Frank & Pat Pleich
416-822-6574
Open 10-5 daily.
Antiques & fine furniture, glass, silver,
China, jewellery, collectibles, dining,
Bedroom & living room furniture.

NEWMARKET
MAPLEVIEW FARM ANTIQUES
3122 Vivian Road, R.R. #3   L3Y 4W1
Dianne & Ralph Gibson
905-836-6339
E-mail: dgibson@interhop.net
htt://peterwebit.com@antiques
Come by chance or phone ahead.
Coutry pine & collectibles,
Refinishing.

OAKVILLE
GRAHAM JONES ANTIQUES
342 Kerr Street   L6K 3B8
Graham Jones FNAWCC
905-849-7881; Fax: 905-825-0092
E-mail: jones@ica.net
10-5:30 Tuesday thru Saturday.
Antique clocks, barometers, banks, toys.
Repairs, buy and sell.

OAKVILLE
OLDE OAKVILLE ANTIQUES
342 Lakeshore Road East   L6J 1J6
Jo Zegers
905-842-6022 (bus.); 905-528-1581 (res.)
Open daily, Sundays by appointment.
Fine selection of traditional & country antiques.
Jewellery, china, glass & nostalgia.

OAKVILLE
THE OAK TILL ANTIQUE
& CURIOSITY SHOPPE
362A Kerr Street   L6K 3B8
Kim Thompson
905-844-7027
11-5:30 Tuesday thru Saturday.
Canadiana & period furniture &
Accessories. Pine & other woods.
Specializing in local Oakville memorabilia.

OAKVILLE
OAKVILLE ANTIQUE MALL
364-366 Kerr Street   L6K 3B8
Lucie & Addy Brings
905-339-3801; Fax: 905-339-2252
Website: www.egocable.net/~antique/
E-mail: Lucie or Addy@oakvilleantique@home.net
10-5:30 Monday, Tuesday, Thursday, Friday,
10-5 Saturday, 12-5 Sunday.
Antique treasures of the world.

OAKVILLE
OAKVILLE USED FURNITURE & ANTIQUES
386 Kerr Street   L6K 3B8
Dan and Donalee
905-845-0961
10-5:30 Mon., Tues., Thurs., Fri., Sat.,
Closed Wed. & Sun.
Antiques, traditional & modern furniture.
China, crystal, paintings, some primitives.
Estates bought, large or small.

OAKVILLE
SQUARE NAILS ANTIQUES
370 Kerr Street   L6K 3B8
Ron, Karl, Mike
905-337-2310
Open 7 days.
We buy and sell antiques,
Books, furniture and collectibles.
Free parking.

ORANGEVILLE
19TH ANNUAL ANTIQUE SHOW & SALE
Agricultural Coliseum & Curling Rink
Fifth Avenue, Orangeville.
Friday, August 18th, 2000, 5-9;
Saturday, August 19, 2000, 10-6;
Sunday, August 20th, 2000, 11-4.
Sponsored by Headwaters Health Care
Centre Auxiliary.
Admission $4 – Held annually in August.

Cookstown Castle Antiques Centre

Your Home Is Your Castle Our Treasures Await You...

We warmly invite you to attend our daily show and sale of precious antiques and collectibles in a medieval atmosphere. With our twenty new vendor displays this is sure to be a unique stop while antiquing in Cookstown

Open Daily 10 a.m. - 5 p.m.
Plenty of Parking Available

Located at northeast corner of the traffic lights on Hwy. 27 at Hwy. 89

7 King St. North, Cookstown
(705) 458-0836

COOKSTOWN ANTIQUE and ART CENTRE

Housed in one of the oldest buildings in the district

Dating back to the mid 19th century

• OPEN SEVEN DAYS A WEEK •
• WE BUY AND SELL •

Quality & Variety

- • *Incredible Antiques*
- • *Unusual Collectibles*
- • *Jewellery*
- • *Exquisite Art*
- • *Silver Cutlery*
- • *Military*

10 Queen Street • Cookstown • Box 255 • L0L 1L0
Telephone: **(705) 458-0903** *(day)*
(705) 458-2345 *(eve)*

ROADSHOW ANTIQUES COOKSTOWN

N.E. corner of Hwy. 400 at Hwy. 89 (Cookstown exit)

*Featuring over 30,000 sq. ft. of Quality Antiques, Fine Art, Collectibles and Memorabilia making this **UNIQUE** haven on of Canada's largest antique centres.*

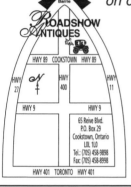

Summer	Winter (Jan.-March)
10 am - 6 pm, Mon. - Fri.	11 am - 6 pm, Mon. - Fri.
9 am - 6 pm, Sat. - Sun.	9 am - 6 pm, Sat. & Sun.

Research Library - Lounge Area
Playroom in Snack & Beverage Section

65 Reive Blvd. - Tel. (705) 458-9898

*Also be sure to visit The Barn at Fowlers Corners
See page 177.*

We Buy & Sell Antiques

WILL SILK'S GENERAL STORE

Antiques & Collectibles, Fudge, Penny Candy, Wrought Iron, Gourmet Foods

OPEN SEVEN DAYS
14 Queen Street
Cookstown, Ontario L0L 1L0
(705) 458-9212
Proprietors: **Laurie & Glen Munroe**

Cookstown Antique Market

Take a drive in the country and visit our 6,000 square foot beautiful barn and shop in air conditioned comfort.

Furniture • China • Glass
Jewellery • Nostalgia • Primitives
Collectibles of all kinds
Vintage Linens & Lace

Displayed by 40 dealers

Located on Hwy. 27, 1 Km. north of Hwy. 89,
5 minutes from Hwy. 400

Open 7 Days A Week

The ongoing
ANTIQUES & COLLECTIBLES SHOW...

Phone: (705) 458-1275
Fax: (905) 458-1847
www.yellow.ca/on/cookstown1.html
Sally & Gerry Robinson

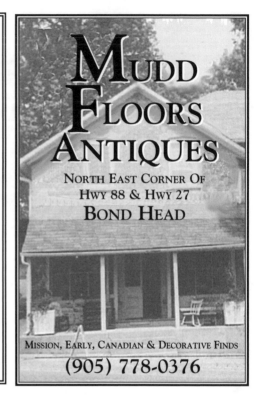

ORANGEVILLE
COUNTRY MANOR ANTIQUES
207535 Hwy. #9 at Conc. 4 Mono
R.R. #5 Orangeville   L9W 2Z2
Barry & Cheryl Spalding-Brand, 519-942-4977
9-5 most weekends,
Weekdays by chance – a call ahead is advised.
Quality primitives, Victorian,
Turn of the century furniture.
Restoration and refinishing.

QUEENSVILLE
THE CAT'S MEOW
R.R. #1, Box 246   L0G 1R0
10 km north of Newmarket
20907 Leslie Street (Sutton Road)
Don & Flo Lewis
905-478-1450
Open by chance or appointment.
Antiques & collectibles.

RICHMOND HILL
MACBETH ANTIQUES &
FINE FURNITURE, INC.
556 Edward Ave., #79 & 80   L4C 9Y5
905-770-5080
Keir Todd
quality oak pieces from Britain.
Mahogany, desks, suites, etc.
Custom refinishing & repairs.
Please phone for appointment.

RICHMOND HILL
WATERFORD WEDGWOOD CANADA INC.
20 West Beaver Creek Road   L4B 3L6
905-886-6400; Fax: 905-886-6532
The Wedgwood International Society
Welcomes your membership.
For information, please call.

ROSEMONT
DUFFERIN COUNTY MUSEUM & ARCHIVES
Corner Hwy. 89 & Airport Road
Box 120   L0N 1R0
Open daily 10-5, closed Monday in winter.
Displays of Dufferin County artifacts.
Special exhibits including Cornflower
Glass by W.J. Hughes.

ROSEMONT
DUFFERIN COUNTY MUSEUM
Antique Show & Sale
Corner Hwy. 89 & Airport Road
Box 120   L0N 1R0
November 10-12, 2000.
Friday, the 10th, 7-10 (preview reception),
Saturday, the 11th, 10-4,
Sunday, the 12th, 12-5.
Held annually.

SCHOMBERG
DE RUITERS MILL ANTIQUES
214 Main Street   L0G 1T0
Sharon Dykstein
905-939-4582; Fax: 905-775-9563
E-mail: www.dykstein@aol.com
10-5 Tuesday thru Saturday,
12-5 Sunday. Closed Monday.
Antiques, gifts, nostalgia, jewellery,
Women's clothing, furniture refinishing.

SCHOMBERG
LINTON LANE ANTIQUES
15325 Hwy. 27, R.R #1   L0G 1T0
Nancy and Mike Dockrill
905-939-7986
By chance or appointment.
Canadiana – early primitives,
Furniture and accessories.

STOUFFVILLE
JOHN LORD'S BOOKS
New location, see Goodwood, Area Map 12
John Lord
905-640-3579
Open 9-5:30 Tuesday thru Thursday
9-8 Friday, 9-5 Saturday, 10-4 Sunday.
Antique & collectible books.

STOUFFVILLE
WILSON ANTIQUES
R.R. #2 13898 Hyw, #48 just north of
The Bloomington Side road   L4A 7X3
905-640-8280
9-5 Monday thru Friday,
10-4 Sunday & Saturday by chance.
Country furniture & collectables.
Restoration • Repairs • Refinishing.

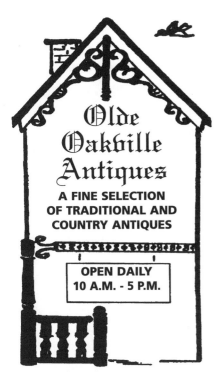

Olde Oakville Antiques

**A FINE SELECTION
OF TRADITIONAL AND
COUNTRY ANTIQUES**

**OPEN DAILY
10 A.M. - 5 P.M.**

**342 Lakeshore Road East
905-842-6022 Bus.
905-528-1581 Res.**

**THORNTON
THE VILLAGE INN**
P.o. Box 27, on Hwy. 27   L0L 2N0
6 Miles south of Barrie
Don Hiles
705-458-9565
Open 10-10 daily.
Steaks & antiques.

**UNIONVILLE
THE GLASS CHIMNEY ART - ANTIQUES**
151 Main Street   L3R 2G8
905-479-3410
11-5 Tuesday thru Saturday, 12-5 Sunday,
Winter shorter hours; please phone.
Extensive selection of china, pressed glass,
Art glass, unique furniture & primitives.
Displayed in five lovely rooms.
Dealers welcome.

**UNIONVILLE
THE JUG & BASIN ANTIQUES**
209 Main Street   L3R 2G8
905-477-3185
Melanie Stone
11-5 Monday thru Saturday, 12-5 Sunday.
Antique china, glass, silver, linens,
Estate jewellery, period English &
Canadian furiture, "Old & Odd Things".
A Family Business, est. 1969.

**STREETSVILLE
NO DIP FURNITURE STRIPPING**
208 Emby Drive, Unit 3   L5M 1H6
Car Saunders
905-826-2002
Open 9-5 Monday, Wednesday & Friday,
9-8 Tuesday & Thursday.
We finish the stripping you started.
Over 30 years in Streetsville.

**UNIONVILLE
THE STIVER HOUSE GIFTS LTD.**
206 Main Street, beside arena   L3R 2G9
905-477-1585
Website: www.stiverhouse.com
Open 11-5 daily. Closed Monday in winter.
Wide selection of excellent Canadiana pine
Furniture. Gifts & crafts from across Canada
& Beyond. Decoys, prints, quilts, etc.
A store with distinction.

**STREETSVILLE
SOME OTHER TIME ANTIQUES**
27 Pearl Street   L5M 1X1
905-826-4657
Website: www.someothertime.com
10-5 Monday thru Saturday,
Closed Sundays.
Specializing in early Canadian furniture,
Pottery, textiles,
Tole and pewter.

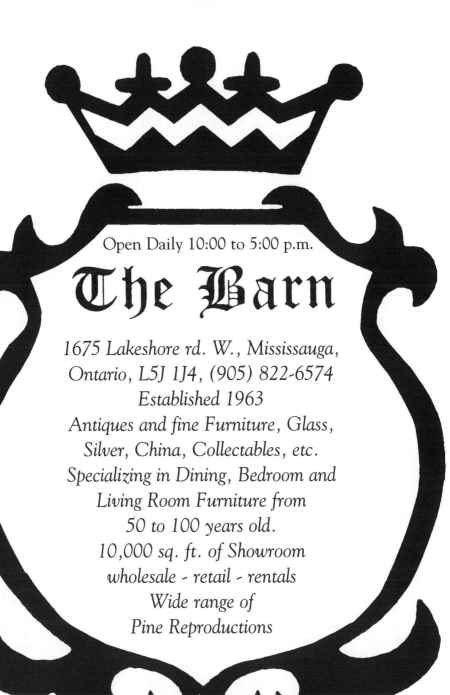

Open Daily 10:00 to 5:00 p.m.

The Barn

1675 Lakeshore rd. W., Mississauga,
Ontario, L5J 1J4, (905) 822-6574
Established 1963
Antiques and fine Furniture, Glass,
Silver, China, Collectables, etc.
Specializing in Dining, Bedroom and
Living Room Furniture from
50 to 100 years old.
10,000 sq. ft. of Showroom
wholesale - retail - rentals
Wide range of
Pine Reproductions

BRITISH HALLMARKS

British hallmarks have acted as a safeguard to purchasers of gold and silver articles for more than 600 years. In 1975 they were extended to platinum, necessitating the introduction of a special Standard mark (the orb surmounted by a cross). It is an offense for any trader to sell or describe an article as gold, silver or platinum unless it has been hallmarked (there are exceptions, including items made before 1900 mainly of gold and/or silver in which the gold is not less than 375 parts in a 1000 and the silver not less than 800 parts in a 1000, and which has not since 1900 been subject to alteration that would have been improper on a previously hallmarked article; gold items weighing less than 1 gram; silver items weighing less than 7.78 grams; platinum items weighing less than 0.5 grams; stone-set gold rings; platinum articles made before 1975).

How do hallmarks protect you?

The hallmark on an article shows that it has been tested (assayed) at an official Assay Office and that the metal conforms to one of the legal standards of fineness or purity. The Assay Offices in Britain are incorporated by royal charter or by statute and all are independent of any trade organization.

What information do hallmarks give?
a. The Sponsor's Mark

This indicates the manufacturer or sponsor of the article. In Britain the mark consists of the initials of the person or firm involved.

b. The Standard Mark

This denotes that the precious metal content of the alloy from which the article is made is not less than the standard indicated. The legal standards and the minimum content of precious metal by weight in parts per thousand are as follows:

22 carat Gold:	916.6	(91.66%)
18 carat Gold:	750	(75%)
14 carat Gold:	585	(58.5%)
9 carat Gold:	375	(37.5%)
Britannia Silver:	958.4	(95.84%)
Sterling Silver:	925	(92.5%)
Platinum	950	(95%)

c. The Assay Office Mark

This identifies the particular Assay Office at which the article was tested and marked. There are now 4 British Assay Offices, in London, Birmingham, Sheffield and Edinburgh. In former times there were others (see later).

d. The Date Letter

This indicates the year in which the article was hallmarked.

How to recognize a hallmark

The example which follows shows a complete Silver hallmark. Although the designs of individual marks have changed from time to time this gives a good idea of what to look for. It shows the sponsor's mark (AB), the mark for Sterling Silver (lion), the London Assay Office mark (leopard's head), and the date letter for 1976 (B).

On Gold articles the standard mark has an additional element denoting the gold content. On 9 and 14 carat articles it comprises the carat rating and the corresponding parts per thousand of gold (see below), ie 9.375 and 14.585; on 18 and 22 carat articles there is a crown (a thistle if marked in Scotland) and just the carat rating figures, ie 18 or 22. As from 1975 the carat rating has not been used, all gold articles bearing the crown or thistle and the figures for parts of gold per thousand.

Standard and Assay Office marks

As most readers of this book are likely to be interested in the earlier marks, we illustrate only the pre-1975 marks.

Prior to 1975	Standard
	22 carat gold Marked in England
	Marked in Scotland
	18 carat gold Marked in England
	Marked in Scotland
	14 carat gold
	9 carat gold
	Sterling silver Marked in England
	Marked in Scotland
	Britannia silver

Prior to 1975	Assay Office
gold & Sterling silver Britannia silver	London
gold silver	Birmingham
gold silver	Sheffield
gold & silver	Edinburgh

Notes – (i) some variations in the surrounding shields are found before 1976. (ii) All Assay Offices mark Britannia silver, but only London (prior to 1975) had a special Assay Office mark for this standard.

GOEBEL

W. Goebel Porcelain Factory, Rodenthal, Bavaria, (West) Germany. Established 1876, made porcelain and earthenware etc. In 1934 introduced figurines based on the drawings of Sister Hummel.

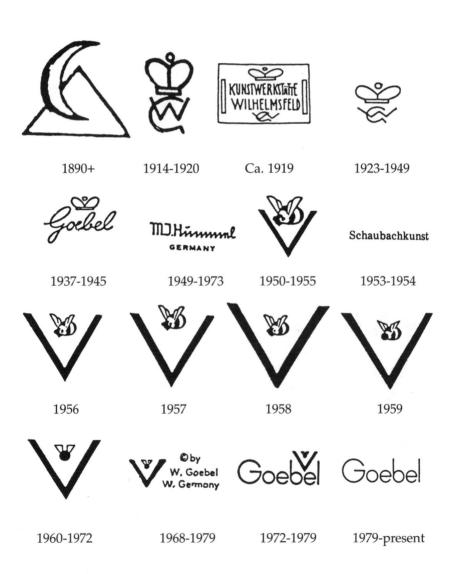

1890+	1914-1920	Ca. 1919	1923-1949
1937-1945	1949-1973	1950-1955	Schaubachkunst 1953-1954
1956	1957	1958	1959
1960-1972	1968-1979	1972-1979	1979-present

DRESDEN

The "Dresden" mark is found on many pieces of porcelain in the Meissen style manufactured since the 1800s. For centuries potteries and porcelain decorators have been established in and near Dresden, Germany. A selection of the many known marks are illustrated.

DECORATOR MARKS: DRESDEN, GERMANY

Hamman, Ca. 1866   Richard Klemm 1869-1916

Donath, 1872+   Used by several decorators – 1883-1893   Lamm 1887+

Wolfsohn, Late 1800s.
Wolfsohn copied the Augustus Rex mark (left) until an injunction ordered her to cease in 1883.

Meyers & Son, Late 1800s

Hirsch, 20th Century

The Willow Pattern

The Willow pattern was originally derived from the Chinese. Early versions vary a good deal but unless they are marked it is virtually impossible to attribute them to any particular maker. By the first decade of the 19th century a standard pattern emerged which has been used ever since.

It is generally accepted that Thomas Minton engraved the earliest pattern with a willow tree when he was apprenticed to Thomas Turner at the Caughley porcelain factory. He later moved to London where he is said to have engraved copper plates for Josiah Spode. In 1799 he set up in Stoke-on-Trent as a freelance designer and engraver. There can be little doubt that many of the line-engraved designs in the Chinese style which were used by the early Straffordshire makers of blue-printed wares were supplied by Minton. Indeed, several of these early prints are very like designs on Caughley porcelain.

Almost all of the very early versions are either unmarked or marked only with small blue-printed symbols which do not help with attribution. The commonest of these are a small eight-pointed star and a little leaf spray. One early design, despite the fact that it includes a willow tree, is normally called the Two Figures pattern.

The name Willow pattern is now generally applied to a standard design which emerged in the first decade of the 19th century and became very popular in Victorian times. Indeed, it is still produced today. It shows a pagoda with pavilion or tea house on the right, backed by an apple tree. In the centre a willow tree leans over a three-arched bridge across which three figures are crossing to the left. In the top left a covered boat crewed by one man floats in front of a small island, and two doves fly in the sky. In the foreground of the design there is a zig-zag fence. There are very many variations on the basic theme.

The Willow Pattern Legend

The standard Willow pattern was extremely popular and legends grew up around the design. These differ considerably in detail but essentially the story concerns a Chinese mandarin, Li-Chi, who lived in a pagoda beneath an apple tree. He had a beautiful daughter, Koong-Shee, who was to marry an elderly merchant named Ta Jin. However, she fell in love with her father's secretary, Chang, who was dismissed when it was discovered that they had been having clandestine meetings. Koong-Shee and Chang then eloped and, helped by the mandarin's gardener, they are seen crossing the bridge which spans the river. The boat is used to approach Chang's house but the furious mandarin discovers their retreat. They are pursued and about to be beaten to death when the Gods take pity on them and turn them into a pair of doves.

A different version of the tale states that the three figures on the bridge are Koong-Shee carrying a distaff, a symbol of virginity, Chang carrying a box of jewels, and Li-Chi, the mandarin, in pursuit with his whip.

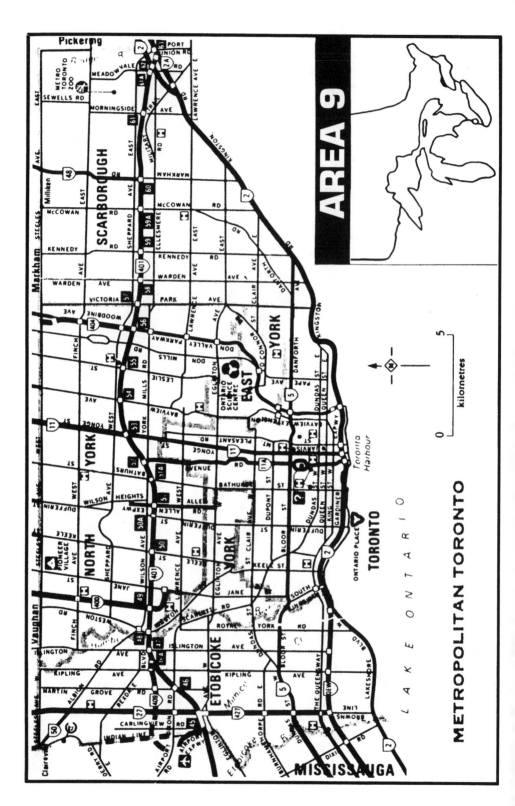

AREA 9

METROPOLITAN TORONTO

Vintage *Style*

Come and See What's New Again!

HARBOURFRONT **Antique MARKET** TORONTO

**100 Dealers and Experts
2 Hours Free Parking**

Tel: (416) 260-2626
Fax: (416) 260-1212
www.hfam.com

390 Queen's Quay West
Every Tuesday through Sunday 10am-6pm

Andrew Richens
Antiques
&
the Dining Room Shop

*The best in fine Mahogany dining room furniture
from our extensive selection...
Plus a good selection of lighting, mirrors, silver
and blue & white transfer ware.*

613 Mount Pleasant Road
Toronto, Ontario M4S 2M5
(416) 487-4437

McLean Ribbehege Antiques

18th and 19th Century English & Continental Formal & Country Furniture,
Porcelain, Silver and Decorative Accessories

604 Mt. Pleasant Rd., Tor., Ont. M4S 2M8 Tel. (416) 489-6517 Fax (416) 489-8892

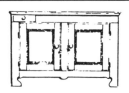

TORONTO
ACANTHUS ANTIQUES
612 Mount Pleasant Road   M4S 2M8
Monika Idler, Douglas Stocks
416-483-8510
Open 10:30-5:30 Monday thru Saturday.
18th & 19th Century formal furniture,
19th Century ceramics &decorative itmes,
Textiles, Canadiana, white ironstone.

TORONTO
ANOTHER MAN'S POISON
29 McCaul Street   M5T 1V7
Hollis G. Landauer
416-593-6451
E-mail: amp99@idirect.com
Large worldwide stock of books on
Antiques, collectibles, & design.
Search service. Special order service.
Out of print titles bought.

TORONTO
ANDREW RICHENS ANTIQUES &
THE DINING ROOM SHOP
613 Mount Pleasant Road   M4S 2N4
416-487-4437
10:30-5 Tuesday thru Saturday, winter,
Monday thru Friday, summer.
Mahogany dining room furniture in
Georgian styles, blue & white transferware.
Chandeliers & silver.

TORONTO
ANTIQUEST
VERITY ANTIQUES INC.
1258 Yonge Street   M4T 1W5
Katrina Wilson
416-972-9841; Fax: 416-964-1894
11-5 Monday thru Saturday, 1-4 Sunday.
Fine antiques from the
19th Century to include furniture,
Decorative items & jewellery.

TORONTO
ADDISON'S INC.
41 Wabash Avenue   M6R 1N1
Jim Addison
416-539-0612, Fax: 416-539-9144
Antique & reproduction
Plumbing fixtures,
Hot water radiators
Architectural artifacts.
Restoration & repairs.

TORONTO
ANTIQUE AID
187A Queen Street East   M5A 1S2
416-368-9565. Call anytime.
11-4:30 Tuesday thru Saturday.
Antique & estate jewellery, porcelain &
Estate jewellery, silver, crystal,
Brass, antique & traditional furniture.
Repairs to porcelain, glass, silver
& Furniture.

TORONTO
ALEX'S ANTIQUE CLOCKS
AND WATCH REPAIRS
465 Manor Road at Bayview   M4S 1T3
Alex Dutescu
416-322-0687
Open 10-6 Monday thru Saturday.
Clocks & watchs, professional repairs
to all makes. European specialist, 40 years
Experience. Personal service – guarantees.

TORONTO
ANTIQUE QUEST
Mary Odette
lady2@home.com
416-429-5591
shows or by appointment.
Victorian glass, china & silver.
Depression glass & collectibles.
Art pottery & Royal Winton.
Mission oak furniture.

TORONTO
ANTIQUE MIRROR RE-SILVERING
SECURITY MIRROR INDUSTRIES, LTD.
69 Densley Avenue   M6M 2P5
416-244-3393, Toll free: 1-800-633-1988
Monday thru Friday.
Tamper-resistant mirrors, antique mirro
Silver, re-silvering, cut mirror & glass.
Detection mirros.
Shower/tub & closet enclosures.

TORONTO
ATTENBOROUGH'S MILITARY
ANTIQUES TRADING POST
1097 O'Connor Drive   M4B 2T5
A.J. Clayton
416-285-6828
Open 9-5 Mondary thru Saturday
Or by appointment.
Everything relating to
Military antiquities.

TORONTO
BERGDON GALLERIES LTD.
180 Davenport Road   M5R 1J2
416-924-3865 or 416-920-7663
11-5 Tuesday thru Friday,
11-4 Saturday,
sculpture, objects d'art,
Antiques.

TORONTO
BERNARDI'S ANTIQUES
699 Mt. Pleasant Road   M4S 2N4
Grace, Paul & David Zammit
416-483-6471, Fax: 483-6849.
11-5 Monday thru Saturday.
Antiques - art - collectibles.
Bought & sold, including
Fine furniture, Moorcroft pottery,
Paintings, bronzes, Doulton, silver.

TORONTO
BIRDS OF PARADISE LAMPSHADES
114 Sherbourne Street   M5A 2R2
Studio: 3rd floor
416-366-4067
appointment recommended.
Designers & makers of quality
Lampshades, in silk, parchment & mica.
Recovering and restoration service.

TORONTO
BLUE ANTIQUES
Harbourfront Antique Market
390 Queens Quay West   M5B 3A6
416-260-5813, Fax: 416-260-1212.
Georgian & Victorian English
Silver, French porcelains,
Crystal decanters & glasses,
Old paintings & prints,
Objects d'art & collectibles.

TORONTO
BREWSTER'S ANTIQUES
56 Wayland Avenue   M4E 3C9
Tim Brewster
416-691-4941
Show sales &
By appointment.
Fine English porcelain.

TORONTO
BRITANNIA SILVERSMITHS
101 Dynamic Drive, Unit 6
Scarborough   M1V 3C9
416-298-8579, Fax: 416-298-1539.
Art Edmonds - Repair consultant
Specialists in silverplating,
Sterling silver. Repairs -
Restoration - polishing brass -
Stainless steel - copper.

TORONTO
CROWN SILVER PLATING CO.
3891 Chesswood Drive,
Downsview   M3J 3C2
Harry Logan
416-636-2995
Open 8-5 Monday thru Friday, 10-3 Saturday
Friday & Saturday 9-1:30 (July, Aug. Sept.)
Replating, repairing &
Polishing of silverware.

TORNTO
CYNTHIA FINDLAY ANTIQUES
Harbourfront Antiques Market
390 Queens Quay West   M5V 3A6
416-260-9057
Website: www.cynthiafindlay.com
Estate jewellery, sterling, art glass,
Objects d'Art, Royal Crown Derby,
Discontinued Royal Doulton figurines
& Tobies, Moorcroft, Belleek, Hummels.
Buy – Sell single items & collections.

TORONTO
DECORUM DECORATIVE FINDS
1210 Yonge Street   M4T 1W1
416-966-6829; Fax: 416-966-0699
10-6 Monday thru Saturday.
Decorative finds.
French & English antiques, fine furniture,
Decorative lighting & accessories.
"Best of the City" – Toronto Life.

TORONTO
DICKINSON GALLERY
1914 Avenue Road, North York   M5M 4A1
Pat and Matt Bustos
416-781-4988
Fax: 416-781-0870
10-5 Saturday and Monday
10-6 Tuesday thru Friday
Specializing in antique prints,
Maps, original watercolours & custom framing.

TORONTO
ETHEL

20th Century Living
1122 Queen Street East   M4M 1K8
Greg Perras & Craig Soper
416-778-6608
12-6 Tuesday thru Sunday,
Closed Monday.
Mid-century furnishings (1930s - '70s)
Rare design pieces for any room.

TORONTO
FINIALS

719 Mount Pleasant Road   M4S 2N4
Ann Stubbs & David Price
416-481-7588
11-5:30 Monday thru Saturday.
Period furniture,
Paintings, decorative arts.

TORONTO
FLOYD & RITA'S ANTIQUES

Harbourfront Market, Shop 3
390 queens Quay West   M5V 3A6
416-260-9066
Open six days, closed Monday.
Banquet lamps, sterling flatware,
Art glass, bronzes, ladies & gents
Jewellery, early light fixtures, inkwells,
Prints, oils & watercolours, toys & dolls.

TORONTO
HARBOURFRONT ANTIQUE MARKET

390 Queens Quay West   M5V 3A6
Canada's largest permanent antique market
416-260-2626
Open six days week, closed Monday.
100 Permanent dealers. Free admission.
Sunday outdoor market May thru September.
Antiques, collectibles.
Exciting selection for all.

TORONTO
HERITAGE ANTIQUE JEWELLERY
and ART GALLERY

Harbourfront Antique Market
390 Queens Quay West   M5V 3A6
Director: Tatiana Kuchinsky
416-26-0398 or 967-1785.
Objects 'dart, paintings
& Antique furnishings.

TORONTO
HERITAGE ANTIQUE MARKET

Bayview Village Shopping Centre
2901 Bayview Avenue, at Sheppard
Just north of Jwy. 401
Monthly antique show & sale, 10-5.
Usually 2nd Sunday in month.
Over 60 dealers from Ontario and Quebec.
Hertiage Antique Sows.
416-483-6471.

TORONTO
INQUISITIVE LTD.

1646 Bayview Avenue
Two blocks south of Eglinton   M4G 2C2
Fritz Lev
416-481-8819
Open 10-6 Monday thru Saturday,
& Friday until 9 p.m.
antique furnishings from Britain & Europe.
Decorative & curio items.

TORONTO
JAN'S GIFT SHOP

319 Sutherland Drive   M4G 1J6
John Morawiec
416-421-9177.
10-6 Tuesday thru Friday, 9-5 Saturday.
closed Sunday & Monday.
Glass repairs, crystal engraving,
Doulton, Kaiser & Lladro figurines,
Crystal, glass, etc.

TORONTO
JOURNEY'S END ANTIQUES LTD.

612 Markham Street   M6G 2L8
One block west of Bathurst, just south of Bloor.
Brian dodge, 416-436-2226 or 536-2301
Open 10:30-6 Monday thru Saturday.
Evenings by appointment.
Sundays & most holidays, 12-5.
Estate Hallmarked, sterling & plated
Holloware & flatware. Furniture, china, etc.

TORONTO
KINGSMEN ANTIQUE RESTORATION

19 Passmore Avenue, Unite 28
Scarborough   M1V 4T5
Peter H. Yeung, 416-291-8939
Open 8:30-5:30 Monday thru Friday,
Other times by appointment.
Invisible meding of art objects.
Prompt – Professional – Personal.
Serving Canada coast to coast.

Old Fashioned Restoration

3068 Dundas Street West
Toronto Ontario M6P 1Z7
Tel: (416) 767-6989

Subject to prior sale

Specializing in Antique Furniture and French Polishing

• Over 25 Years Experience in Genuine Antique Furniture Restoration and French Polishing
for Antique Dealers, Galleries and Private Collectors

• We also Deal in Buying and Selling Georgian, Victorian, Edwardian and Unusual Pieces

• For a Free Estimate call Emanuel (Lee) Calleja or visit our Display
at 3068 Dundas Street West and see our Selection of European Antiques

OPEN MONDAY TO SATURDAY 9:00 A.M. TO 6:00 P.M.

WEST TORONTO JUNCTION
Treasures...of Time

Antiques,
Collectibles and
Decorative Items
"We Buy, Sell and
Take Consignments"

3075 Dundas St., W. Toronto, Ontario M6P 1Z5
(416) 766-0802

 **Plus Two More Exciting Antique Stores Nearby**

TORONTO
KRAYEVSKY STUDIO
Conservation & Restoration
Harbourfront Antique Market
390 Queens Quay West   M5B 3A6
Oleg & Ariadna Krayevsky
416-260-2626 or 416-789-1837 (eves)
125 Years of family tradition,
30 Years experience as restorers and
Conservators of antiques & family treasures.

TORONTO
MOBILE ANTIQUE SHOWS
40 Metropolitan Road, Unite #34
Scarborough   M1R 2T6
416-200-9951, Fax: 613-232-7424.
Antique shows promoted
Throughout Ontario.
Watch Antique Showcase magazine
For dates and locations.

TORONTO
LORENZ ANTIQUES LTD.
701 Mount Pleasant Road   M4S 2N4
Lorenze, Irene & Isabel Biricz
416-487-2066; Fax: 416-487-9264
9:30-5 Monday thru Friday,
10-4:30 Saturday.
Fine period furniture and
Objects of art.
Member of C.A.D.A.

TORONTO
MONTGOMERY'S INN
4709 Dundas Street West
Etobicoke   M9A 1A8
416-394-8113
9:30-4:30 Monday thru Friday,
1-5 Saturday, Sunday & Holidays.
City of Etobicoke Museum –
An historic inn restored to the 1840s.

TORONTO
**LUDGE MICIULEVICIUS – FINE
ANTIQUES & DECORATIVE ARTS**
Victoria & Ludge Miciulevicius
416-781-3168
By appointment only.
Exhibitors at major antique shows.
Continental & English period
Furniture, chandeliers,
Silver & objects d'art.

TORONTO
NADIA'S ANTIQUES
581 Mount Pleasant Road   M4S 2M5
(South of Manor)
416-486-6621
Usually open Tuesday thru Saturday.
A beautiful selection of
European porcelain,
Antique dolls, clocks,
Furniture & lighting.

TORNTO
MANLEY & SHEPPARD ANTIQUES
Tim Manley & James Sheppard
416-385-1784
At major shows or by appointment.
English & European porcelain,
Glass, silver, Orientalia,
Bronzes, fine furniture,
Paintings & rugs.

TORONTO
NORTHERN TIME INC.
238 Davenport Road, Suite 292   M5S 2T2
Steven Oltuski
416-323-1905 days/evenings.
E-mail: watches@northerntime.com
Specializing in buying & selling
Fine wristwatches &
Antique jewellery.

TORONTO
MCLEAN & RIBBEHEGE
604 Mount Pleasant Road   M4S 2M8
Sharon McLean, Roland Ribbehege
416-489-6517; Fax: 416-489-8892
10:30-5:3- Monday thru Saturday
Or by appointment.
Specializing in 18th and 19th century English
And Continental furniture, porcelain, silver
And decorative accesories, including great
Iron and marble consoles.

TORONTO
OLD CHINA PATTERNS LIMITED
1560 Brimley Road at Ellesmere
Scarborough   M1P 3G9
Glen Roe, Don Roe
416-299-8880, Toll Free 1-800-663-4533.
8:30-5 Monday thru Thursday,
8:30-4:30 Friday.
Discontinued china & crystal bought & sold.

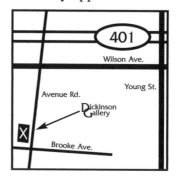

TORONTO
OLD FASHIONED RESTORATION
3068 Dundas Street West   M6P 1Z7
E. Lee Calleja
416-767-6989
9-6 Monday thru Saturday,
Appointment preferred.
Specializing in antique furniture
& French polishing. Over 25 years of
Experience in furniture restoration.

TORONTO
J.E. O'NEIL ANTIQUES, LTD.
100 Avenue road   M5R 2H3
June E. O'Neil
416-968-2805
11-5 Monday thru Saturday.
Quality Canadian
Country furniture and
Accessories.

TORONTO
PACKAGING STORE
660 Eglinton Avenue East   M4G 2K2
416-485-6562, FAx: 416-485-6797
E-mail: pack@idirect.com
Edward Perdue
custom packaging and crating,
Multiple shipping options,
On-site estimates, pick-up service,
Packaging materials, insured shipments.

TORONTO
PACKAGING STORE
24 The East Mall, Etobicoke   M8W 5W5
Edward Perdue
416-201-4441; Fax: 416-201-4442
E-mail: pack@idirect.com
Custom packaging and crating,
Multiple shipping options,
On-site estimates, pick-up service,
Packaging materials, insured shipments.

TORONTO
PALETTE FINE ART GALLERY
(Formerly Classic Art Restorations)
1260 Yong Street   M4T 1W5
Kostas Xenarios, Helen Chialtas, Lisa Cohen
416-968-9000; Fax: 416-968-6662
10-6 Monday, Tuesday, Wednesday & Friday,
10-7 Thursday, 10-5 Saturday.
Restoration of paintings, frames, & china.
Custom framing and sales of original art.

TORONTO
PAM FERRAZZUTTI
Harbourfrount Antqiue Market
390 Queen's Quay West   M5V 3A6
416-639-2608 or 260-0325
Quality Majolica – Hundreds
Of pieces in stock.
Always interested in purchasing.
Antiques bought and sold.

TORONTO
PAT DILLION ANTIQUES
AND TOY SOLDIER CENTRE
Harbourfront Antique Market
390 Queen's Quay West   M5V 3A6
Booth G-3
Home: 416-266-0241, Bus.: 416-260-9087,
Fax: 416-266-0241.
E-mail: pdantique@globalserve.net
Website: www.patdillon.com
Toy soldiers, jewellery, silver.

TORONTO
R.G. PERKINS & SON ANTIQUES
1198 Yonge Street   M4T 1W1
Bob &Sheldon Perkins
Tel./Fax: 416-925-0973, Toll free: 888-475-5868
E-mail: perkins.group@sympatico.ca
10:30-6 Monday thru Friday,
10:30-5 Saturday.
Canadian country furniture & accessories.

TORONTO
PHILLIP'S LAMP SHADES LTD.
172 Main Street   M4E 2W1
416-691-7372
9-5 Wednesday thru Friday,
10-4 Saturday. Closed Monday & Tuesday.
Parts, fittings, glassware for
Oil & electric lamps & fixtures.
Repair & service.
Catalogue: $5.50.

TORONTO
PICKWICK'S CHOICE
1698 Queens Street West   M6R 1B3
Harold & Audrey Barrett
416-538-4419
10-6 Monday thru Saturday.
Antiques & accessories.
We buy – Please call.

TORONTO
D. PLATT PROMOTIONS INC.
4 Greenacres Road   M6M 4A7
Doug Platt
416-653-0864
Producers of "Another Time"
Antique Shows. See monthly
Magazine for display advertising
& Calendar of shows.

TORONTO
SOME OTHER TIME ANTIQUES
27 Pearl St., Streetsville   L5M 1X1
David Hamilton Wells
905-826-4657
Website: www.someothertime.com
10-5 Monday thru Saturday,
Closed Sunday.
Specializing in early Canadian
Furniture, pottery, textiles,
Tole & pewter.

TORONTO
PLUM'S EMPORIUM LTD.
107 Miranda Avenue   M6B 3W8
416-782-9135, Fax: 416-782-6478
Web page: www.plumsemporium.com
9-5 Monday thru Friday, 10-5 Saturday.
Architectural & decorative antiques,
British, European & Oriental furniture,
Pictures, pottery, procelain, lamps,
Restaurant theme deocr & props.

TORONTO
SUSAN'S ANTIQUES
585 Mount Pleasant Road   M4S 2M5
Susan Miller
416-487-9262
10-5 Monday thru Saturday.
Victorian wicker furniture,
Quilts, silk flowers,
Accessories & other fine antiques.

TORONTO
RITCHIE'S
Auctioneers and Appraisers of
Antiques & Fine Art.
288 King Street East   M5A 1K4
For catalogue for our upcoming
Sales, please contact us at:
416-364-1864, Fax: 416-364-0704.
Misa, MasterCard, A.E. & Interac.

TORONTO
THE BEAD GOES ON
256 Soudan Avenue   M4S 1W4
Off Mount Pleasant, 1 block south of Eglinton
Cyndy Calder
416-481-7622
11-6 Monday thru Saturday.
Antique & costume jewellery
Vintage accessories.
Collectible glass & china.

TORONTO
SARAH GRESHAM ANTIQUES
201 Queen Street East   M5A 1S2
416-865-1758
12-6 Monday thru Saturday
Fine antique lace & linen,
Art glas, photo frames,
Furniture,d ecorative arts,
Silver & jewellery,
Property rentals.

TORONTO
THE CHINA COLLECTION
135 Cartwright Avenue   M6A 1V4
416-256-0041; Fax: 416-256-3551
E-mail: omnisource@sprint.ca
Website: www.thechinacollection.com
10-6 Monday thru Friday,
11-5 Saturday, 12-5 Sunday.
"Town & Country Antiques"
Gathered from the far corners of China,
Tibet, Mongolia and North Korea.

TORONTO
SHARON O'DOWD ANTIQUES
689 Mount Pleasant Road   M5S 2N2
Sharon O'Dowd – 416-322-0927
11-5 Monday thru Saturday.
19th Century Canadiana pine.
Furniture in original paint or
Finely restored.
Own line of country reproductions
Inspired by Quebec & Nova Scotia antiques.

TORONTO
THE DOOR STORE LTD.
43 Britain Street at Queen & Sherbourne
Sam Mirshak   M5A 1R7
416-863-1590
10-5 Monday thru Friday, 10-3 Saturday.
Architectural antiques, stained &
Bevelled glass, fireplace mantles.

TORONTO
THE FIREPLACE
379 Eglinton Avenue West   M5N 1A3
416-483-1143
9:30-5:30 Tuesday thru Saturday.
Mantlepieces, antique &
Reproduction fireplace furnishings.
Victorian & traditional exterior
Lighting in copper, black & white.

TORONTO
THE OLDE TYME CLOCK SHOPPE
1684 Queen Street West   M6R 1D3
John Burke
416-534-8063
10-5 Wednesday thru Saturday.
Specializing in the sale and repair of
Antique clocks.

TORONTO
THE TORONTO VINTAGE CLOTHING AND TEXTILE SHOW & SALE
The Enoch Turner Schoolhouse
106 Trinity Street
Admisson $5, children under 12 free.
March 4, 2001
June C. Troy
905-666-0523 or 905-666-3277.
Vintage clothing & accessories.

TORONTO
THE PAISLEY SHOP LTD.
77 Yorkville Avenue   M5R 1C1
416-923-5830, Fax: 416-923-2694
9-5:30 Monday thru Friday, 10-5 Saturday,
Closed Saturday, June, July & August,
Or by appointment.
18th & 19th Century English furniture,
Porcelain & decorative objects.
Member C.A.D.A.

TORONTO
THE PLANTATION
608 Markham Street   M6G 2L8
Thomas Keeling
416-533-6466
11-6 Monday thru Saturday,
12-4 Sunday, or by chance.
Old jewellery, art glass, cabinet &
Miniature items, Orientalia,
Snuff boxes, bottles.

TORONTO
THE RECYCLISTS
4 Greenacres Road   M6M 4A7
Pam & Doug Platt
416-653-0864
By appointment only.
We buy, sell, trade & repair all makes of
Wind-up phonographs & gramophone,
Cylinder & disc music boxes. Diamond Disc,
Cylinder records bought & sold.

TORONTO
THE STORE ANTIQUES
588 Mount Pleasant Road   M4S 2M8
Peter Griffiths
416-483-2366
A wide variety of antiques, clocks,
Canadian pine, Claphams' beeswax
Products & antiwax.

TORONTO
THE VILLAGE BOOK STORE
239 Queen Street West   M5V 1Z4
416-598-4097
10-9 Monday thru Friday,
10-6 Saturday & Sunday.
Reference books for
Antique collectors.

TORONTO
TREASURES... OF TIME
3075 Dundas Street West   M6P 1Z5
416-766-0802
11-6 Tuesday thru Friday,
10-5 Saturday.
Antiques, collectibles & decorative items.
Come and find a piece of the past
That you can... treasure.
Buy, sell, take on consignment.

TORONTO
TURN OF THE CENTURY LIGHTING
112 Sherbourne Street
at Richmond   M5A 2R2
S. Walsh & D. Ivens
416-362-6203
10-6 Monday thru Friday,
10-5 Saturday
Fine quality lighting, ca. 1850-1930.
Restoration service.

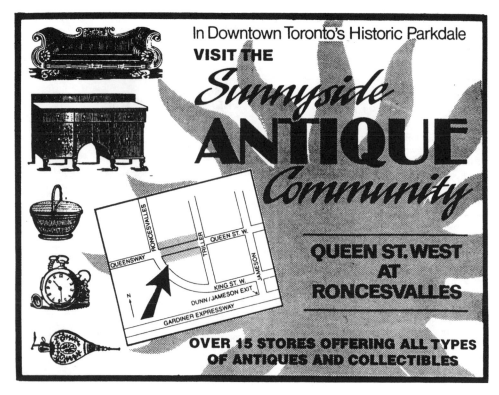

TORONTO
THE SUNNYSIDE ANTIQUE COMMUNITY
QUEEN STREET WEST AT
RONCESVALLES IN DOWNTOWN
TORONTO'S HISTORIC PARKDALE.
OVER 18 STORES OFFERING ALL
TYPES OF ANTIQUES & COLLECTIBLES.

HIDEAWAY ANTIQUES
1605 Queen Street West   M6R 1S9
Bill jarman
416-539-0833
11-6 Wednesday thru Sunday,
Monday & Tuesday by chance
Or appointment.
Buying and selling quality furniture,
Lamps, clocks, etc.

ARCADIA ANTIQUES
1605 Queen Street West   M5R 1A9
Ron Goulet
416-534-0348
11-6 Tuesday thru Sunday,
Closed Monday.
Fine furniture,
Antiques and collectibles.

P. ROUSSELL ANTIQUES
1686 Queen Street West   M6R 1A9
Pamela Roussel
416-534-3833
10:3-4:30 Mon., Wed., Thurs. & Fri.
9:30-6:00 Sat., 11-5 Sun.
Furniture,a rt, mirrors &
Small collectibles.

ERA
1629 Queen Street West   M6R 1A9
Brian Clish & Sale Mosser
10:30-6 Tues. thru Sat., 11:30-6 Sun.
Or by appointment. 416-535-3305
Large assortment of vintage lighting,
Antique furniture and fine decorates
From Canada, U.S.A., England, France,
& Italy. Over 150 late 19th-20th Century
Paintings in stock. – We Buy –

UPPINGTON HOUSE
1605 Queen Street West   M6R 1A9
Dianne Uppington
416-532-0805
12-5 Wednesday thru Sunday.
Antique & vintage textiles,
Linens, clothing, fashion
& Decorative accessories.

TORONTO
UPPER CANADA HOUSE LTD.
467 Eglinton Avenue West   M5N 1A7
Ralph or Jonathon
416-489-9110
10-5 Tuesday thru Saturday.
Closed Saturday July & August.
Antiques & interior design,
Decorative accessories,
Prints & picture frames.

TORONTO
VINTAGE LIGHTING
1150 Castlefield Avenue   M6B 1E9
Off Dufferin Street
5 minutes south of Yorkdale
416-789-1704
Regular hours.
An eclectic array of antique &
Reproduction home accessories & fixtures
Also at 356 Richmond Road, Ottawa,
613-722-1570

TORONTO
WADDINGTON'S
Auctioneers and Appraisers
111 Bathurst Street   M5V 2R1
the Southeast corner at Adelaide
416-504-9100; Fax: 416-504-0033.
Website: www.waddingtonsauctions.com
We specialize in the appraisal & sale of
Antiques and household effects, either
Individual items or entire contents.

TORONTO
WALKER'S ANTIQUES
& SILVER EXCHANGE
Harbourfront Antique Market
390 Queens Quay West   M5B 3A6
Don & Freda Walker at 416-260-9068
After 5 p.m. at 613-352-3646
E-mail: stersilsta@sympatico.ca
Sterling & silverplate pattern
Matching service.
Buy & sell. Porcelain & small furniture.

TORONTO
WHIM ANTIQUES
561 Mount Pleasant Road   M4S 2M5
Mary & Maura McQueen
416-481-4474; Fax: 416-481-1168
E-mail: whimant@interlog.com
Website: www.whimantiques.com
10:30-5:30 Monday thru Saturday
Belleek, jewellery, and
Sterling flatware.

TORONTO
WHIMSY ANTIQUES
597 Mount Pleasant Road   M4S 2M5
Carlo Moro
416-488-0770
10-5 Monday thru Saturday.
Specializing in 19th century
Canadian pine furniture,
Folk art, toleware, treen,
Lamps, china & glass.

TORONTO
LOUIS WINE LTD.
Established 1880
140 Yorkville Avenue   M5R 1C2
Gary & Richard Wine
416-929-9333 Fax: 416-929-9625
Website: www.louiswine.com
10:30-5:30 Mon. thru Fri., 10:30-5 Sat.
Fine antique silver & antique jewellery.
Valuers, purchasers of works of art. Appraisals.

TORONTO
JOHN YOUNG GALLERIES
3317 Yonge Street at Fairlawn   M4N 2L9
John Young
416-482-3317
10-6 Monday thru Saturday, Thursday until 8.
Closed Monday, July & August.
Formal dining room furniture
Desks, commodes, mirrors
& Occasional furniture.

TORONTO
YE OLDE CLOCK DOCTOR
221 Queen Street East   M4E 1E8
Peter Marshall, Esq., M.C.M.
416-439-2312 Fax: 416-439-5932
Antique clock & watch service. Since 1740.
E-mail: pmesq1@net.com.ca
Website: www.toronto.com/yeoldeclockdoc
Buy – Sell – Service – Estimates.
Estate & insurance appraisals.

*A superb pair of mahogany ladder-back side cairs, circa 1780;
a mahogany powdering stand of rare design; and a fine quality
Chippendale gilt and carved wood mirror, 3' 10" high.*

BELLEEK ~ CHINA MARKS

Belleek: Ireland's first and still foremost porcelain, has been prized by collectors for over 100 years. Today, just as in 1857, each piece is made entirely by hand by local craftsmen who take pride in continuing family skills and traditions.

FIRST MARK 1863-1890
This basic trademark features the Irish Wolfhound, one of Ireland's distinctive round towers, and the Irish harp. It was often applied as an ink transfer in black. Sometimes a smaller version was impressed into the base of the ware.

SECOND MARK 1891-1926
The second mark, in black, added a ribbon with the words "Co. Fermanagh, Ireland".

THIRD MARK 1926-1946
The third mark, in black, placed a circular Celtic design and the words "Deanta in Eirinn" (Made in Ireland) and the registered trademark number (0857) below the second mark.

FOURTH MARK 1946-1955
The fourth mark, in green, was identical to the third mark in every way but colour. Green was found to be less likely to show through the translucent parian.

FIFTH MARK 1955-1965
The fifth mark, in green, added a capital letter "R"" enclosed in a circle. This signified that it had been registered in the U.S. Note that since 1955 all marks contain the registration R.

SIXTH MARK 1965-1980
The sixth mark, in green, was reduced in size to make it suitable on smaller articles. The ribbon was shortened to just the word "Ireland" and the U.S. registry symbol was placed immediately above the Irish harp.

On April 1st, 1980 Belleek announced the introduction of a new trademark, its seventh. It is similar in design to the sixth mark, except that the circular Celtic design has been eliminated. The colour has been changed to antique gold, to commemorate the 100th anniversary of the Gold Medal received at the 1880 Melbourne International Exposition.

Belleek ~ The History

The Belleek Works were established in 1857 in Co Fermanagh, Northern Ireland by Caldwell Bloomfield, Robert Williams Armstrong and David McBirney. The distinctive, ultra-thin porcelain was first exhibited at the Dublin Exhibition in 1865 and the factory soon became famous for parian ware ornamental items.

They were often modelled in the form of shells and other marine objects, which were finished with the characteristic iridescent glaze resembling mother-of-pearl. Services and wares of all types were also produced, including open work baskets and vases with extremely fine flower encrustation (made possible by the strength of the parian body), as well as ordinary white china and white graniteware.

The village of Belleek which gave its name to the pottery, was called "Beal Leice" in Gaelic, and referred to the flagstone ford which provided a convenient river crossing at the western end of Lough Erne.

In December 1925 after prolonged political negotiations and "anti-government" violence, the actual boundary was established between the Irish Free State (Eire) and Northern Ireland. This lead, early in 1926, to a significant change in the Belleek mark. (Note the third Black mark).

During the pottery's early years high quality earthenware was its primary product, and much of this can still be found throughout Great Britain and in parts of the USA. The extent of this earthenware ranged widely from kitchen utensils like platters, bowls, basins, jugs and dishes to large items such as hospital and institutional items like bathtubs and toilets and even telegraph insulators. The production of earthenware finally ceased in 1946. Parian china, however, was the pride of the pottery and quickly gained worldwide renown when it won the prestigious gold medal awards in Dublin (1865), Melbourne (1880), Adelaide (1887) and Paris (1900).

The pottery prospered throughout the years, but also endured a number of hard times because of two world wars which limited exports and materials, and various changes in ownership, until in 1990 it was purchased by George Moore, a native of Ireland residing in the USA. George and his wife Angela have pledged to maintain Belleek's traditional superior craftsmanship.

Extra Identifying Marks

During the First Period certain identifying marks were in use on occasional pieces in addition to the regular Belleek trademark. The additional marks may be transfers, but often they are impressed without colour.

On some of the early earthenware the Irish harp or the harp with a crown above it appears to indicate the distinctive material which was used. Rare pieces may be found which have the harp without the Belleek trademark.

The British Registration Mark was used to register the production and the date the piece was shipped to the wholesaler. This registration mark was used on certain pieces until 1883.

Some prominent wholesalers had their company names marked on the base of the parian china which they sold, for example "R.H. Macy and Co. Inc. New York."

Some early pieces were marked with the original name of the pottery "D. McBirney and Co. Belleek". This name may also have been used with the first period trademark.

The name "Belleek" or "Belleek Co. Fermanagh" was impressed without colour on special pieces particularly those with a larger base. After 1891 the name of the country of origin "Ireland" was added to this impressed mark. ✤

Promoters

**Don't Forget to
Advertise your shows!**

~ Notes ~

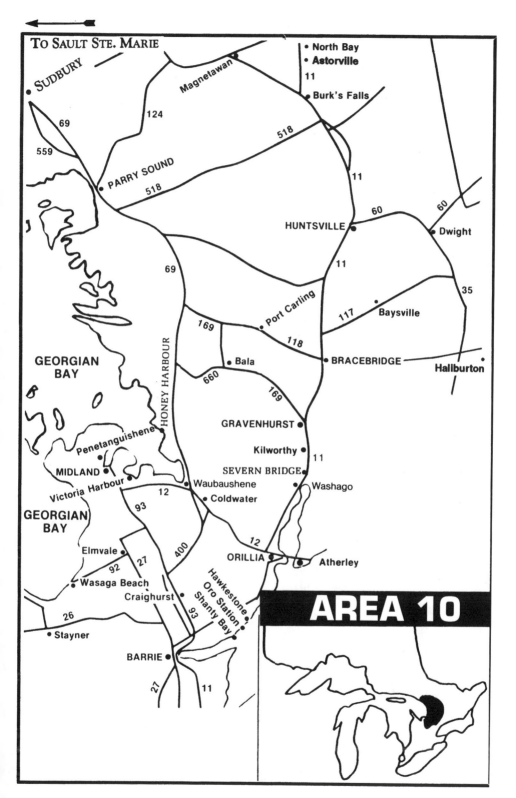

2000–2001

Bala Sports Arena

Antique
Show Sale

June 30th, 2000	6–9
July 1st, 2000	10–5
July 2nd, 2000	11–5
Sept. 30th, 2000	10–5
Oct. 1st, 2000	11–5
June 29th, 2001	6–9
June 30th, 2001	10–5
July 1st, 2001	11–5
Sept. 29th, 2001	10–5
Sept. 30th, 2001	11–5

Admission includes re-entry
$4.00 Opening Night
$3.00 Saturday and Sunday
(Children under 12 free)

Info:
(705) 484-1668

BALA
ANTIQUE SHOW & SALE
Bala Sports Arena
17th Summercade of Colour
June 30th - July 2nd, 2000
Friday, June 30th, 6-9, admission $4;
Saturday, July 1st, 10-5;
Sunday, July 2nd, 11-5.
Admission $3 (children under 12 free)
Admission includes re-entry.

BALA
ANTIQUE SHOW & SALE
Bala Sports Arena
29th Cavalade of Colour
Sat., September 30th, Sun., October 1st, 2000
Admission $3 (children under 12 free).
Info: 705-484-1668.
Admission includes re-entry,
Refreshments available.

BALA
ANTIQUE SHOW & SALE
Bala Sports Arena
18th Summercade of Colour
June 29th - July 1st, 2001
Friday, June 29th, 6-9, admission $4;
Saturday, June 30th, 10-5;
Sunday, July 1st, 11-5.
Admission $3 (children under 12 free)
Admission includes re-entry.

BALA
ANTIQUE SHOW & SALE
Bala Sports Arena
30th Cavalcade of Colour 2001
September 29-30.
Saturday, September 29th, 10-6;
Sunday, September 30th, 11-5.
Admission $3 (children under 12 free)
Info: 705-484-1668
Admission includes re-entry.

BALA
CROW THINGS
Bala Falls Road, Box 222   POC 1A0
angela macdonald, mfa.
705-762-1576
Weekends: May-October.
Daily: July & August, 10-5.
Antiques, art & accessories,
Decorating services.

BARRIE
BARRIE ANTIQUE MALL
272 Innisfil Street   L4N 3G1
705-726-1663
Seven days, year round, 10-6,
Open Friaday & Saturday until 7 p.m.
25,000 Sq. ft. with 120 dealers
Full of antiques, nostalgia and
Collectibles of every kind.
Also sell by Internet auction.

BARRIE
F. BRIGGS, WHOLESALE
THE ANTIQUE CELLAR
264 Coxmill Road   L4N 4G5
F. Briggs
705-722-0084
By appointment or chance.
Antique & art.
Dealers only

BARRIE (SHANTY BAY)
MOMENTS IN TYME
Hwy. #11 North (Gasoline Alley)
Comp. 404, Shanty Bay   L0L 2L0
Raymond & Cecile Bates
705-728-6860
10-Dusk, 7 days.
We buy and sell: Quality used
Furniture, collectibles, estates.

BARRIE
SPRING HOUSE ANTIQUES
R.R. #6   L4M 5P5
Dorren & Don Jewell
705-722-3950
By appointment only.
China, dolls, art & oil lamps.

BAYSVILLE
CROSS/CUT ANTIQUES
18 Bridge Street   P0B 1A0
Barbara Jones
705-767-2500 or 767-3887
Open weekends
Or by chance or appointment.
Early Canadiana & pine furniture,
Memorabilia & collectibles.

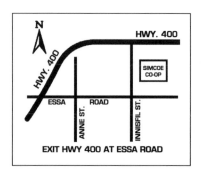

BAYSVILLE
WENDY'S GIFTS 'N THINGS
Bay Street   P0B 1A0
Wendy Maynard
705-767-2181
10-5 Daily in July & August. Weekends April,
May, June, September, October & December.
Antiques, books, collectibles, gifts,
Depression glass.
Old & different.

BRACEBRIDGE
18th ANNUAL 2001
ANTIQUE SHOW & SALE
Bracebridge Arena
Thursday, July 5th 4-9;
Friday, July 6th 11-9;
Saturday, July 7th 11-5.
705-764-0939;
Fax: 705-764-0940.

BRACEBRIDGE
CORDUROY ROAD ANTIQUES
193 Manitoba Street
Michael Beasley, Laura Kendall
705-769-1140 Res.
10-5 Tuesday thru Saturday,
Closed Sunday and Monday,
Other times by chance or appointment.
Antiques, art & collectables
Bought and sold.

BRACEBRIDGE
PAST AND PRESENT ANTIQUES
R.R. #2 (1191)   P1L 1W9
North side of Hwy. #117, 2 km east of Hwy. #11
Katharine & Doug Patterson
705-645-2679, Fax: 705-646-2311
Open year round.
specializing in large & small furniture,
In most woods. Also china, glass
& Collectibles.

BRACEBRIDGE
THE COUNTRY COLLECTION
R.R. #1, Hwy. 118 West   P1L 1W8
Nancy Shier
705-645-9191
Open daily, mid-May thru Thanksgiving.
Three floors of early Canadiana
And accessories.

BRACEBRIDGE
OLD STUFF ANTIQUES & COLLECTIBLES
1833 Hwy. 118 West, 8.5 km from town.
Dee & Liz Denyar
705-645-5386
Spring & fall – weekends,
July & August - Thursday to Sunday 10:30-5,
Monday - Wednesday by chance or
appointment.
Pine country furniture, quilts, mirrors,
Lamps & other accessories.

BRACEBRIDGE
THE MOUSE HOLE
10 Manitoba Street, Box 1585   P1L 1V6
Trudy Niezen
705-645-0177
April-December, Monday - Saturday,
January - March, weekends only.
Antiques and collectibles,
Furniture, jewellery, china, glass.

BRACEBRIDGE
WILDFLOWER ANTIQUES
3 Manitoba Street   P1L 1S4
Josie Savijarvi
705-646-8771 or 764-1954
March thru December, Monday thru Saturday,
10-5:30; July & August, also
Sundays, 12-4; January & February by
appointment. Antique Canadian pine
Furniture, custom made pine reproductions.

BRACEBRIDGE
WORTH REPEATING
27 Manitoba Street   P1L 1S4
Ann & Steve Newroth
705-646-1246
E-mail: worthrep@surenet.net
10-5:30 Monday - Friday, 9-5:30 Saturday,
Open Sunday, May - August.
Quality home furnishings & antiques,
Consigned and sold including home
Accessories - china, clocks, silver, rugs, etc.

GRAVENHURST
DITCHBURN HOUSE
811 Bay Street   P1P 1G7
(opposite Sagamo Park)
1-800-475-2818 or 705-687-2813
Doug & Sharon Smith
Spring: Weekends 10-5:30, Summer: 7 days
1:30-5:30, Fall: Sep. to mid-Oct., 10:30-5:30
(Closed Tues.), Winter: Weekends,
10:30-5:30 (Oct., Nov., Dec.).
Antiques, collectibles, crafts & gifts.

GRAVENHURST
E-Z WAY PRODUCTS CANADA INC.
R.R. 2 Gravenhurst   P1P 1R2
705-687-0729 or 1-800-387-2296
Or 705-721-1137, R.R. 3 Barrie   L4M 2S5
E-Z Way Paint & Varnish Remover, BRIWAX wood
cleaner & polish & metal cleaning & Polishing products. Available at selected Antique, home & wood
shows, or by mail order. Call for show listing or
ordering information.

GRAVENHURST
LISA McCOY WICKER RESTORATION
213 Musquash Road South
P.O. Box 53   P1P 1T5
Lisa McCoy
705-786-8538
Open seven days.
Wicker furniture repairs, chair seating
In cane, splint & rush, canoe
Seats, free estimates.

GRAVENURST
THE OLD LAMPLITER
130 Muskoka Road North,
P.O. Box 1145   P1P 1V4
Sam Comer
705-687-4719
Open 10-5, six days, closed Sundays.
Antique & reproduction lighting specialist
electric & kerosene lampes - repairs,
Sales, parts, and fittings.
Specializing in Aladdin Lamps.

HONEY HARBOUR
BEE HIVE ON THE WATER
Behind the L.C.B.O.
P.O. Box 121   P0E 1E0
Brad Osborne
705-756-2349
Open 9-6 daily from May to mid-October.
Antiques, crafts, gifts &
Summer leisure wear.

HUNTSVILLE
B'S ANTIQUES & THINGS
Lynx Lake Road   P0A 1K0
Al & Frances Botham
Open Saturday & Sunday from Victoria Day
Thru June, 12-6 daily in July & August.
Weekends only from Labor Day to Thanksgiving.
Furniture, tools, glass, china & collectibles.

HUNTSVILLE
B'S 2 HIS & HERS
Lynx Lake Road   P0A 1K0
Al & Frances Botham
Open Saturday & Sunday from Victoria Day
Thru June, 12-6 daily in July & August.
Weekends only from
Labor Day to Thanksgiving.
Fishing, sports & military items.
Toys and coins.

MIDLAND
HURONIA MUSEUM
Little Lake Park   L4R 4P4
director: James Hunter, 705-526-2844
Open: 9-5 Mon. thru Fri.
from April 1 thru May 17; 9-5 Mon. thru Fri.
& Sun. from May 18 thru Oct. 14;
& 9-5 Mon. thru Fri. from Oct. 15 thru Dec. 20.
Simcoe county furniture, tools, dolls,
Ephemera, cloths. Half-million artifacts.

MIDLAND
THE CROW'S NEST
236 King Street   L4R 4K8
705-526-6131, Fax: 526-0744
Open 9-6 all year round, seven days.
Collectibles, giftware, kitchenware,
Jewellery, smoke shop, doll gallery,
Brass, antiques, wicket, pawn, Lottery/Nevada.
Buy - Trade - Sell, cheque cashing.
Also at 61 Mississauga E., Orillia,
705-327-7777.

ORILLIA - ATHERLEY
HINTON'S ANTIQUES
65 Tivnon Lane (Atherley)   L3V 1B8
Just over the bridge from Orillia
Wendy & Stephen Hinton
705-325-9666
E-mail: steve@hintonantiques.com
By appointment only.
Pre-Confederation country furniture.
Estate appraisals,
Restoration, refinishing.

ORILLIA (ATHERLEY)
McKEE RESTORATION
66 Orchard Point Road, Atherley L3V 1C6
705-325-1518
Jim McKee
By appointment only.
Please telephone ahead.
Antique picker – showing "as found."
Also carving Totem poles.

ORILLIA
THOMPSON ANTIQUES
THE LAZY FARMER
P.O.Box 162   L3V 6J3
Located on Hwy. 11, 5 miles north of Orillia
Chris & Danny Thompson
705-325-7262
E-mail: ethings–@things.org
Open most days.
Antiques & collectibles.

ORILLIA
CINDY'S ANTIQUE MALL
& CRAFT SUPPLIES
37 Mississauga Street West   L3V 3A5
Cindy Dubeau
705-325-4088; Fax: 705-326-1236
Open 7 days, year round.
Antiques, collectibles & memorabilia.
Quality dealers – Victorian & Canadian furniture,
China, glass, pottery & ephemera.
Auctions & appraisal services available.

ORILLIA
ORILLIA ANTIQUE MALL
61 Mississauga Street East,
below Crow's Nest
705-329-2118
Open daily in the summer,
Closed on Monday & Tuesday in winter.
Quality dealers featuring: Victorian &
Canadian furniture, fine china & glass,
Primitives, wicker & memorabilia.

PARRY SOUND
HARRIS' ANTIQUES
17 Parry Sound Drive   P2A 2W9
Dean Harris
705-746-5100
9-5 Mon.-Sat. or by appointment.
Restored & rough Canadian furniture,
Custom built oak & pine furnishings.
Complete line of wicker furniture.
New mattresses and sofas.

PARRY SOUND
SO & SO ANTIQUES
14 Bay Street   P2A 1S3
Across from the Isand Queen
Gord Skarott & Jean Weening
705-746-7611
9-5 Seven days,
Summer, June-September open 'til 9 p.m.
Antique furniture and glassware,
Collectibles and custom lamp shades.

PORT CARLING
ANTIQUES AT THE RED BARN
2902 Hwy. #118   P0B 1J0
705-764-3232
Summer Season: daily 11-5,
Shoulder Season: weekends only,
Or by appointment.
Fine antiques and collectibles
From Pollikers, Lowlynds & Hintons'.

SUDBURY
JILL'S ANTIQUES
1935 Paris Street at Plaza 69   P3D 3C6
10-6 Wednesday thru Saturday.
Antique & tribal jewellery,
Vintage clothing & accessories,
Victorian scent bottles and hatpins,
Antique linen & lace.
And always the unusual.

WAUBAUSHENE
WAUBAUSHENE HERITAGE
Coldwater Road at Pine   L0K 2C0
John & Mary Carpenter
705-538-1857
E-mail: wauher@on.aibn.com
Open 11-5 daily from May thru January,
(Closed Wednesdays), winter by chance
Or appointment.
Pottery, decoys, pressed glass,
Candles & furniture.
BED & BREAKFAST.

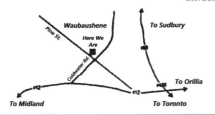

~ Notes ~

Nippon

Royal Crown Derby

Minton

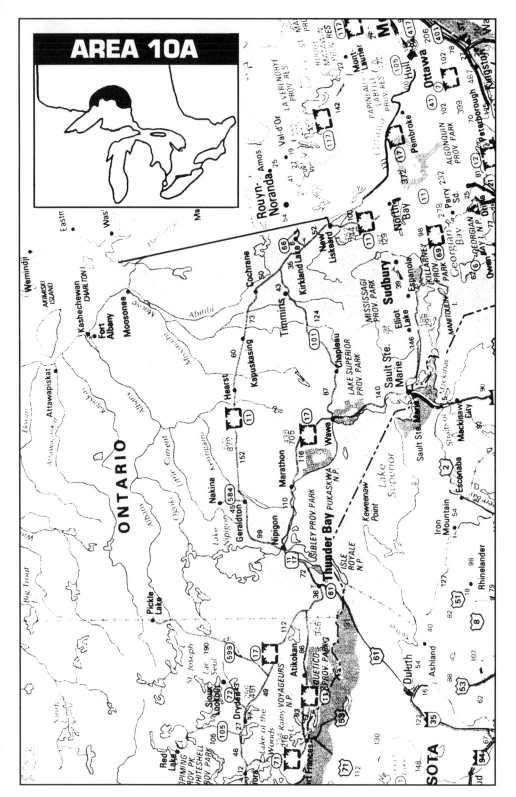

THUNDER BAY
BLACK CAT ANTIQUES
Paul Kimberley, Lee Searles
807-623-5502
E-mail: info@antiquesandrefinishing.com
Website: www.antiquesandrefinishing.com
By appointment only.
Fine antiques, furniture, china,
Glass and jewellery.
Also visit Victoriaville, The Marina,
10 and 20 South Court Street.

THUNDER BAY
LINDA & NORM'S ANTIQUES
& COLLECTIBLES
18 South Cumberland Street   P7B 2T2
Linda & Norman Kuusisto
807-344-1554 Fax: 807-344-6204
10-5 Monday thru Saturday
Furniture, Depression glass, old bottles, toys
China, glassware, jewellery, silverware,
Doulton, Hummel & Beswick figurines.
Railroad memorabilia & lamps.

THUNDER BAY
NORTHERN LIGHT ANTIQUES
20 North Cumberland Street   P7A 4K9
Bev Vass
Tel./Fax: 807-345-0355
10-5 Monday thru Friday,
10-4 Saturday
Glass, brass, china, silver,
Linens, militaria, collectables,
Country and fine furniture.

THUNDER BAY
THE PAPER CHASE
1110 Lakeshroe Drive   P7B 5E4
Wayne & Mary Pettit
Tel./Fax: 807-983-2890
E-mail: paperant@tbaytel.net
Open by chance or appointment
Books, bottles, glass, china,
Magazines, pamphlets, sheet music,
Toys, etc.

THUNDER BAY
VICTORIA'S CUPBOARD
111 North May Street   P7C 3N8
Marjorie Knutson
807-622-7821
10-5 Monday thru Saturday
China, glass, vintage linens and
Clothing, and other
Victorian inspired collectibles.

THOUGHTS TO PONDER

❧

Take time to work ~
it is the price of success.

❧

Take time to think ~
it is the source of power.

❧

Take time to play ~
it is the secret of perpetual youth.

❧

Take time to read ~
it is the fountain of wisdom.

❧

Take time to be friendly ~
it is the road to happiness.

❧

Take time to dream ~
it is hitching your wagon to a star.

❧

Take time to love and be loved ~
It is ordained of God.

❧

Take time to look around ~
the day is too short to be selfish.

❧

Take time to laugh ~
it is the music of the soul.

AN OLD IRISH PRAYER

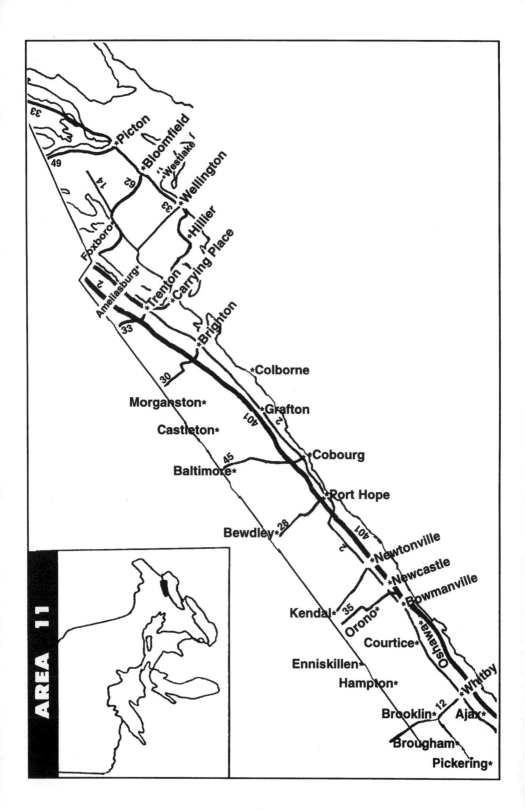

AJAX – PICKERING VILLAGE
ANTIKA ANTIQUES
109 Old Kingston Road   L1T 3A6
Unit 6 "The Courtyard"
Lisa and Ray Ataergin
905-426-2888
E-mail: sales@antika.ca
Website: www.antika.ca
10:30-5 Tuesday thru Sunday.
Good quality formal furniture, china & glass.

AJAX – PICKERING VILLAGE
ANTIQUE DISCOVERIES
78 Old Kingston Road
Pickering Village   L1T 2Z8
905-683-8243 Fax: 905-426-6140
Jeff Clark
Come visit our new barn.
Tuesday thru Sunday, Monday by chance.
Quality collectibles,
Restoration & refinishing.

AJAX – PICKERING VILLAGE
GODIVA ANTIQUES & GIFTS INC.
22 Linton Avenue   L1T 2X5
Pat & Gord Haughton
416-683-1018
Closed Monday.
Victorian & Canadiana
Furniture, primitives, glas & china.
Country store & craft items.

AMELIABURGH
GRANNY'S ATTIC ANTIQUES
"The Furniture Doctor"
County Road #2, south of Ameliasburgh
613-969-8298   K0K 1A0
10-5 Most days,
June 1st thru November 1st.
Primitives, oak country furniture,
Dolls, Teddy's, glass & china.

BOWMANVILLE
ANTIQUES BY THE LAKE
25 Bennett Road, R.R. #4   L1C 3K5
Reid & Debby Allin
905-697-3539
Open by chance.
Country furniture &
Decorating accessories.

BOWMANVILLE
THE BOTTOM DRAWER /
JUST MY IMAGINATION
2936 Hwy. #2, east of Bowmanville
Bill Lankhof / Karen Cashin
905-623-4509
10-7 Thursday thru Sunday.
Antiques, art, collectibles.
Will help you locate items, or
Sell your items on commission.

BOWMANVILLE
DAYS OF FUTURE & PAST ANTIQUES
1546 Taunton Road East,
Hampton   L0B 1J0
David & Brenda Hughes
905-432-3896
10-5 Saturdays, Sundays & Holidays
Or by appointment during week.
Iron beds with brass trim,
Mahogany and walnut furniture.

BRIGHTON
THE BREAKAWAY ANTIQUES
R.R. #7 (Guertin Road)   K0K 1H0
4 km. north of 401 on Hwy. #30
Jill & Bud Guertin
613-475-2671
By chance or apointment.
Furniture mostly in the rough,
And old postcards.

BROOKLIN
THE BROOKLIN ANTIQUARIAN
47 Baldwin Street, Hwy. #12   L0B 1C0
David Stewart
905-655-3723
Open by chance or appointment.
Refinished country furniture
And accessories.

BROUGHAM
HARVEST ANTIQUES LIQUIDATORS
Hwy. 37 & Brock Road North
David & Brenda Hughes
905-427-9670 / 905-432-3896 (res.)
10-5 Friday thru Monday.
Come & visit 4,000 sq. ft. showroom.
Mahogany and walnut diners, bedrooms.
Accessories, fine china,
Restored antique lighting.

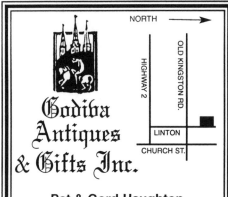

CARRYING PLACE
KLINGSPON'S DRIVE-SHED ANTIQUES
P.O.Box 43, Hwy. #33 south from
Hwy. #2 to Country Road #64,
First house west of post office   K0K 1L0
Marie Klingspon
613-392-5771
Open Saturday, closed Sunday,
Other days by chance or appointment.
Cranberry & general antiques.

CARRYING PLACE
THE FINAL TOUCH
R.R. #1, Rednersville Road on the bay
613-962-4073   K0K 1L0
Open mid-april thru November.
By chance or appointment.
Eclectic collection of
Hand-picked antiques.

CASTLETON – MORGANSTON
COBBING ANTIQUES
& COLLECTABLES
R.R. #1 Castleton, P.O. Box 16,
Junction of County Rds. 25 & 27
West of Hwy. #30
905-344-7840   K0K 1M0
By chance or appointment.
19th & 20th Century period furniture.
Glass, china, & estate jewellery.
Also furniture caning.

COBOURG
COBOURG BOOK ROOM & ANTIQUES
150 King Street West
Brian & Kathy Harling
905-373-8868
9-5 Monday thru Saturday; 12-4 Sunday.
Glass & porcelains.
Specializing in Belleek & Shelley,
English furniture, decorative
Arts, books & art.

COLBORNE
OLDE SEATON HOUSE ANTIQUES
& COLLECTABLES
Box #32, 57 King Street East   K0K 1S0
Robert Ian Anderson
905-355-1804
9-6 Wednesday thru Sunday.
Period & Canadian furniture, home
Accessories, framed prints, gardening,
Craft & decorating books.

ENNISKILLEN
S.B.W. HORSE & CARRIAGE ANTIQUES
1893 Regional Road 3, R.R. #1
905-263-2275   L0B 1J0
Bill & Sonja White
10-6 Sunday. Saturday & evenings
By chance or appointment.
Specializing in old hanging &
Other type lamps, clocks, furniture,
& Horse-drawn carriages & sleighs.

FOXBORO
THE COUNTRY CORNER SHOP
R.R. #1, corner of Hwys. #14 & 62
Robert Vandebelt
613-969-0731
Open seven days.
Furniture refinishing,
Collectibles & tools.

GRAFTON
BINGHLEY HOUSE ANTIQUES
168 Aird Street   K0K 2G0
(Between Hwy. 401 & Hwy. 2)
Luke Verroken
905-349-3126
Open by chance, 11-5.
Fine English, Continental, and
North American furniture.
Decorative lamps, vases, silver, etc.

GRAFTON
1812 ANTIQUES & GARDENS
105 Old Danforth Road   K0K 2G0
905-349-3756
10-5 Daily, 12-5 Sunday.
Garden open holiday weekends.
English formal, country furniture,
Decorative accessories, local
Wrought iron.
Pick your own bouquets.

GRAFTON
THE TOLE LANTERN
105 B Old Danforth Road   K0K 2G0
905-349-3889
Lyn De La Cour
10-5 Daily, closed Wednesday,
Sunday by chance.
Unique, vintage and modern lighting,
Unusual custom shades, wonderful finials,
Decorative accessories.
Always something different.

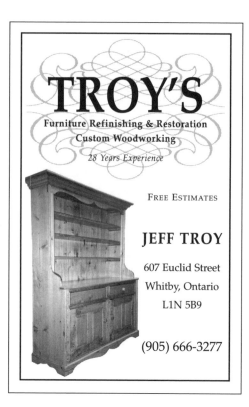
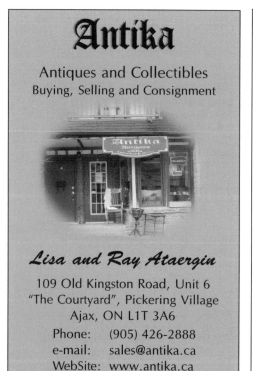

GRAFTON
ST. JOHN'S BOOKS
105B Old Danforth Road   K0K 2G0
905-349-3743
Janis Attard
10-5 Daily, 12-5 Sunday, closed Wednesday.
Specializing in gardening, cooking,
Decorating, craft, nature and children's books.
Distinctive cards & stationery.
Elegant gift wraps & accessories.

GRAFTON
SPAULDING'S INN & ANTIQUES
10715 County Road #2
SW corner of #2 & Brimley Road
P.O. Box 10   K0K 2G0
Morse & Jane Goddard
416-349-2816 (res.)
Open daily.
Antiques, collectibles & jewellery.
An eclectic collection.

MILFORD
PAST REFLECTIONS
3026 County Road #10
Between post office & Milford Ice
613-476-8003 – Box 4   K0K 2P0
Fred & Freda Spice
10-5 Daily May thru October,
10-5 Thursday thru Sunday, October thur May.
Antiques & collectibles,
Furniture stripping, refinishing & supplies.

NEWCASTLE
DAN STURROCK CABINETMAKER
236 King Street West   L1H 1C7
416-987-4489
Open by chance.
A call ahead is advisable.
Custom pine furniture &
Accessories for the
Country home & garden.

PICKERING
PICKERING ANTIQUE MARKET
Metro East Trade Centre
1899 Brock Road   L1V 4H7
Contact: Anne Seli
905-427-0754
8-5 Sundays – Free I.D. clinic
"We cater to the collector."
Over 70 dealers with antiques,
Collectibles, toys, art & more.

PICTON
HOUSE OF FALCONER ANTIQUES
190 Main Street, Box 353   K0K 2T0
Thera Falconer
613-476-5635 (bus.) or 613-476-2875
By appointment.
Fine antique furniture,
China & gass.
"A thing of Beauty is a Joy Forever."

PICTON
LOYALIST ANTIQUES & FINE ART
R.R. #1 Loyalist Pkwy., 1 km.
East of Bloomfield   K0K 2T0
Christopher & Norah Rogers
613-393-2728
By chance or appointment.
18th & 19th Century formal &
Country furniture & accessories,
Fine Canadian art.

PORT HOPE
GANARASKA PICKERS MARKET – ANTIQUE MALL
50 John Street   L1A 2Z2
David Hamayda
905-885-7979; toll free: 1-877-775-7979
10-5 Seven days.
22 Dealers offering wide selection of
Country and formal furnishings.
Glass, china, toys, porcelain, iron,
Retro, arts and crafts, pottery.

PORT HOPE
HINCHCLIFFE & LEE ANTIQUES
136 Walton Street   L1A 1N5
Jack and Carolyn Lowry
905-885-5905
Fax: 905-377-9068
11-5 Seven Days
Closed in winter.
Oriental antiques from China.

PORT HOPE
LEE CASWELL ANTIQUES INC.
60 Walton Street   L1A 1N1
905-885-1118; Fax/home: 905-885-9443
Lee Caswell   1-877-346-6586
11-5 Tuesday thru Saturday,
12-4 Sunday. Phone ahead always advised.
Specializing in fine quality
18th to 20th century decorative antiques
For the discerning collector.
Designers & trade always welcome.

PORT HOPE
SMITH'S CREEK ANTIQUES
27 Walton Street   L1A 1M8
Beside the river.
Carol & Clay Benson – Member C.A.D.A.
905-885-7840
Open seven days.
Two floors of antiques.
Specializing in Canadiana as well as
Decorative and period furnishings.

PORT HOPE
THE MANOR ON WALTON
127 Walton Street   L1A 1N4
Brent Bayley, Jennifer Wetherall
905-885-0155
11-5 Seven days – Summer
11-5 Thursday thru Monday – Winter
Tuesday & Wednesday by appointment.
Victorian & Edwardian furniture & accessories.
Team Room – Luncheons & Afternoon Teas.

PORT HOPE
UPTOWNE ANTIQUES
246 Ridout Street   L1A 1P3
Steven & Laurie Goldiuk
416-885-0190
Open 6 days.
Wednesday by chance or appointment.
Wide selection of antiques,
Vintage clothing, lighting, clocks.
Fresh stock weekly.

PORT HOPE
VINTAGE CLOCKS
127 Walton Street   L1A 1N4
Brent Bayley – Horologist
905-885-0115
11-5 Seven days – Summer
11-5 Thursday thru Monday – Winter
Tuesday & Wednesday by appointment.
Buy and sell clocks & barometers.
Repairs & restorations on premises.
Over 100 clocks in stock.

TRENTON
IRENE'S ANTIQUES
R.R. #4, Hwy. Stn. Main   K8V 5P7
#33 South
Irene Markvart
613-392-3924
9-6 Daily, closed Monday.
Fine antiques &
The unusual.

WHITBY
BAYBERRY'S
126 Brock Street South   L1N 4J8
905-666-8420 – Julie Kuiper
10-5 Tuesday thru Saturday.
Antiques, gifts, fine clothing,
Primitive pine & reproductions.
Woolrich, Suttles & Seawind Designs.
Yankee candles, Native Canadian.
Limited edition fashion tops.

WHITBY
LAFONTAINE TRADING POST
106 Dundas Street West   L1N 2L9
Barbara Power & Sisters
905-430-3774
10-5:30 Monday thru Saturday.
Distinctive old time shopping.
Antiques, reproductions, and jewellery.
Exciting clothings.

WHITBY
TROY'S FURNITURE RE-FINISHING
AND RESTORATION
607 Euclid Street   L1N 5B9
905-666-3277
Jeff & Melinda Troy
Monday thru Saturday.
Custom sprayed finishing &
Custom woodworking available.
Free estimates.

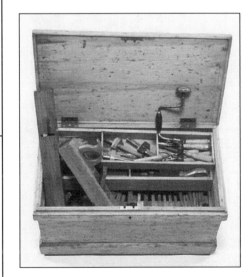

WOODSTOVES HAVE AN INTERESTING HISTORY

Almost every home or cottage in Muskoka has a least one fireplace or woodstove. The history of the fireplace goes back as far as the human use of fire, but the history of stoves is surprisingly recent.

The English with their more moderate climate, have always favoured fireplaces. When the German and Scandinavian colonists first came to North America, they knew a bit more about cold weather and brought with them what were state-of-the-art woodstoves.

The Lennard fireback.
1636 Brighton Museum.

Most of those were simply rectangular cast iron plates which bolted together to form a box. The interesting thing about those early stoves was that they used just five cast plates. There was no back; they had only a top, bottom, two sides and a front, and were aptly called "Five Plate" stoves.

When bolted together, the box was placed against a wall with a hole in it.

On the other side of the wall was the kitchen fireplace, used for all the cooking. Hot coals could be pushed through from the kitchen into the stove, providing some warmth to the room where the stove was located. Only a single central chimney was needed. The cast iron box was normally supported on stones or pottery, about 14 inches off the floor.

European cast iron stove plates date from about the mid to late 15th century, or about the time of Luther or

Columbus. They were, of course, a luxury and available only to the upper classes. These early stoves were commonly decorated with elaborate motifs from the Bible.

The early American colonists had access to plenty of fuel and soon found deposits of iron ore in Pennsylvania and New Jersey. Small furnaces or foundries were established and the first simple stove plates were cast in North America about 1726.

The process consumed huge quantities of wood however, and coal deposits had yet to be discovered. The supply of wood was quickly depleted for miles around and few of these early furnaces survived for more than a very few years.

Many of the American stove plates were exact copies of imported European plates, but in some cases new wooden patterns were carved. The carvers were evidently not highly skilled since reverse printing is commonplace. Decorations were copied from the only books available – usually the Bible or Aesop's Fables.

Sometime about 1760, the first "Six Plate" stoves appeared. These had a back in them so that they could sit out in the room. Some had both a hinged front door and a circular opening in the top through which smoke could be piped to the main chimney. These "Six Plate" stoves would seem familiar to most of us today. We might assume the modern woodstove is simply a direct version of those first "Six Plate" stoves – but that's not the case.

Cooking ranges with a distinctly Victorian flavour on sale in the era of Art Deco,
Catalogue of the Army & Navy Stores, London, for 1928.

Examples of the early "Six Plate" stoves are in fact exceedingly rare. They were manufactured for only about four years. It took just that short time for some bright furnace master to design and build the much more popular "Ten Plate" stove.

The "Ten Plate" stove had a cavity on its side – a sort of box within a box. The great advantage of this arrangement was that you could bake bread or pies, or roast meat, without having the food covered in ashes.

The "Six Plate" stove was eclipsed immediately. Relatively few had been made and some of those were discarded for the new and improved model.

It was not until much later, with refinements similar to the modern cookstove, that box stoves came back into vogue for the parlor. Early "Six Plate" are a true collector's item and the very few which survive are in the museums.

During this same period cast firebacks were commonly installed in the fireplaces. These flat plates were thought to reflect more heat into the room. Reproductions of those early firebacks ar available again today. They add a unique touch of the past to the modern fireplace. The active use of firebacks continued until about 1830. A few of the "Five Plate" stoves were manufactured until 1770, but then they too disappeared.

Benjamin Franklin's stove was invented in 1742. The original had no front door, so it was actually a fireplace rather than a stove. It was considerably different and more complex than the thing we think of as a Franklin stove today. There was a double back, or baffle, so that the smoke was forced back down near the base of the stove before it could escape up the chimney. Unless the chimney was very good, these Franklin fireplaces tended to smoke badly.

During the last 15 years we have experienced another period of rapid change in the design of stoves. Here in Canada the steel woodstove is more popular than cast iron. There is no difference in the heating properties of the two materials, but cast iron will withstand the higher temperatures generated by some coal fires. There is relatively little coal used as a stove fuel in Canada, so the choice is largely one of design preference by the owner.

There is now a strong movement towards higher efficiency and stoves which produce fewer particles in their emissions. These more sophisticated stoves can also be much more demanding in terms of their operation, the chimney systems they require, and their need for careful maintenance.

Functional differences between stoves have become increasingly important but are not well understood by most owners. Muskoka is a woodburning area where both the warmth and esthetic values of a woodfire will remain popular for many years.

GEORGE V
&
QUEEN MARY
SILVER JUBILEE 1935
TWENTY-FIVE YEARS

From 1784 to 1890 the Sovereign's head always appeared as part of the legal hallmark stamped by the Assay Office on silver to denote the payment of duty. Only on one occasion has the Assay Offices ever used the head of the Sovereign and his Queen, this was when it was agreed to commemorate the Silver Jubilee of their Royal Majesties King George V and Queen Mary. This mark was used from 1933/4 to 1935/6.

Arthur Tremayne, the well-known authority on clocks, watches, diamonds and silver was the originator of the idea and went to a great deal of trouble to get it put into effect. In fact before the mark could be used, the laws of England had to be changed and not only did the Goldsmith's Company, provincial Assay Office, Board of Trade, The Mint and Treasury have to be convinced and give their approval, but the Home

Office sanction had to be waited for. The original of the obverse side of the official Jubilee Medal (designed by Mr. Percy Metcalf) was used for the punch.

This was a very exciting event in the history of silver for in more than six centuries of hallmarking it had never been used as anything but a mark of high quality for precious metals; never before had it been linked with events of national importance. Certainly it was the first time two crowned heads appeared on any stamp used for marking silver articles.

This fact alone makes any piece with the Jubilee mark of considerable importance. Samples can be found today, as thousands of sets of spoons, six to the set, each bearing the mark of a different Assay Office, were made and sold. The British Industries Fair sold many pieces to both home and overseas buyers, so you can be certain that Canada received its share. Many items: tea-services, trays, coffee pots, vases, flatware, boxes, etc., were so marked and are definitely worth looking for as an addition to a collection of silver or Royal Commemoratives.

GEORGE V & QUEEN MARY SILVER JUBILEE
Town Marks & Date Letters

Town Mark	1933-4	1934-5	1935-6
London	8	t	U
Birmingham	J	K	L
Sheffield	q	r	s
Chester	b	d	k
Glasgow	K	l	m
Edinburgh	C	D	E

- 174 -

China Language

(NC) – When registering or shopping for china, you should become familiar with tableware terms. Royal Doulton provides the following glossary:

Place setting: Most formal five-piece settings consist of one each of – dinner plate, salad plate, bread & butter plate, teacup and saucer. Casual dinnerware may come in four-piece place settings made up of – dinner plate, salad plate, soup/cereal bowl and mug. Ask the place-setting components before comparing prices.

Open stock: This term is perhaps the most misunderstood. It means that you will be able to buy pieces of your china pattern individually such as the saucer without the teacup.

Service plate: May also be referred to as a Charger plate. This is an oversized decorative plate which is usually set at the table under the dinner plate.

Fine bone china: A ceramic body comprised of china clay, stone and bone ash. Despite its translucent appearance it is remarkably strong.

Fine china: A ceramic body which does not contain bone ash and therefore is generally opaque and less expensive but nearly as strong as bone china.

Backstamp: The stamp on the base of china which indicates the manufacturer, country of origin and generally the pattern name.

For further information on the vocabulary of china, contact Royal Doulton Canada Limited at 1-800-268-4040.

Caring for your china

(NC) – You've probably spent hours selecting your new china pattern with visions of intimate dinners à deux or perhaps huge family get-togethers. So why do so many people keep it "safely" stored in their china cabinet? The experts at Royal Doulton, one of the world's most popular brands, advises that china is stronger than most people think. "In fact, bone china is the most durable, ceramic body available, despite its delicate appearance," states Shona McLeod, Public Relations Manager for Royal Doulton Canada Limited. The following do's and don'ts will ensure a long-lasting relationship with your new china.

- Do ask which dishwashing detergents are recommended by the manufacturer. Most dinnerware is completely dishwasher safe following using these products.
- Do rinse food off before placing in the dishwasher.
- Don't slide wet plates over one another when rinsing. China is most susceptible to scratching by other pieces.
- Do rotate your dinnerware to ensure that pieces are used equally.
- Do stack plates with a paper napkin between them to protect from scratches.
- Don't place too many plates on one another to create a heavy stack.
- Don't stack teacups inside one another. Store on their base or suspend them by their handles on hooks.
- Don't subject china to extreme change in temperature. Never place on an open flame.
- Do enjoy your china frequently. You selected it, so enjoy!

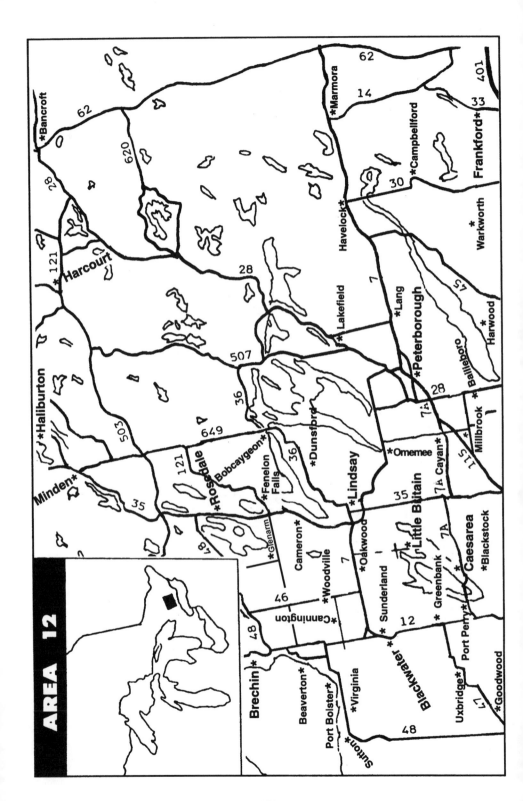

AREA 12

Bancroft*
62
620
28
121
Harcourt*
Haliburton*
Minden*
503
35
121
Rosedale*
Bobcaygeon*
649
Fenelon Falls*
36
48
Glenarm*
Cameron*
Woodville*
46
Cannington*
48
Brechin*
Beaverton*
Port Bolster*
Virginia*
Sutton*
48
Blackwater
Sunderland*
12
Uxbridge*
Goodwood*
7
Port Perry*
Caesarea*
Blackstock*
7A
Greenbank*
Little Britain
35
7A Cayan*
Omemee*
Lindsay*
Oakwood*
7
Dunsford*
507
36
28
Lakefield*
Havelock*
7
Lang*
Peterborough*
Bailieboro*
Harwood*
45
Warkworth*
30
Campbellford*
Frankford*
33
401
Marmora*
14
62
Millbrook*
115
28
7A

- 176 -

ROADSHOW ANTIQUES COOKSTOWN

Presents

NEW   NEW

Antiques
at the
B A R N

Fowlers Corners, Peterborough

**Up to 20,000 sq. ft. Well Known Facility
at the Crossroads of Hwy. 7 at 7B (Cty. Rd. 1)**

**Tel: 705-740-2452 Fax: 705-740-0148
www.roadshowantiquesmall.com**

**Fowlers Corners is the gateway to the Kawartha Lakes
estimated tourist traffice over 4 million yearly.
Fowlers Corners is situated on the outskirts of
Peterborough and Lindsay, population of 100,000
25 minutes from Hwy. 401.
Near Port Hope another Antique hot spot.**

**Operated and Managed by
ROADSHOW ANTIQUES COOKSTOWN**

DEALER INQUIRIES WELCOME

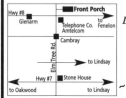

BEAVERTON
BEAVER HOUSE ANTIQUES
414 Simcoe Street   L0K 1A0
Thelma Willis & Barbara Brayshaw
705-426-9558
11-6 daily, year round.
Antiques & collectibles.
Special blend of old &
Not-so old.
Something for everyone.

BEAVERTON
MORTSON'S
R.R. #3   K0K 1A0
West side of Hwy. 12/48
4 miles north of Beaverton.
Bernice Mortson
705-426-9075
Usually open 7 days.
Antiques & collectibles.
Lawn & patio furniture.

BEAVERTON
THE COMMODORE
R.R. #1   L0K 1A0
7 km. south of Beaverton,
4 km north of Port Bolster on Durhan Rd. 23
(Lakeridge Road).
Adam & Donna Dobson
705-426-4601
E-mail: adobson@accel.net
9-5 Monday thru Saturday, 12-5 Sunday.
Antiques, gifts, collectibles, reproductions,
Custom built furniture & refinishing.

BEAVERTON
THE CURIOSITY SHOPPE
Regional Road #23
Lakeridge Road, Port bolster
Pat Teel
705-437-2544
Weekends or by chance.
"Old fashioned as the Dickens"
Antiques 'n things.

BLACKWATER
BLACKWATER BRIC-A-BRAC SHOPPE
R.R. #4, P.O. Box 9   L0C 1H0
Right on Hwy. 7/12
Bill Mann
705-357-1099
Open daily.
Bric-A-Brac
Antiques, curiosities &
Collectibles.

BRECHIN
THE PROUD HERITAGE
ANTIQUES AND DESCENDANTS
P.O. Box 70   L0K 1B0
Barbara & Peter Sutton-Smith
705-484-1668
Major show exhibitors only.
English & European porcelain,
18th & 19th Century copper & brass,
Victorian art glass, silver.

CAMERON
CAMERON SCHOOL HOUSE ANTIQUES
Hwy. 35 North, 11 km. north of Lindsay
Kathie & David Simpson
705-359-1199
Open six days.
Closed Mondays.
Large selection of antiques & collectibles.
Specializing in oil lamps.

CANNINGTON
EBOR HOUSE ANTIQUES
157 Cameron Street East   L0E 1E0
Bill & Gwen King
705-432-2655
10-5:30, six days,
Closed Mondays.
Oak, walnut & mahogany furniture,
China, collectibles and
Refinishing.

CANNINGTON
VICTORIANA ANTIQUES
& COLLECTABLES
C. 1755 Saginaw (Cameron St.)   L0E 1E0
705-432-1010
Josephine Peters
By chance or appointment.
Antiques, collectables & gifts.
Buy, sell & trade.

FENELON FALLS
THE WAY WE WERE
95 Colborne Street   L0M 1N0
Pam Armstrong
705-887-3035
10-5 daily May 1 thru October 31,
11-6 Sunday,
Other times by chance.
Canadiana, pine, primitives "original colour."
Garden accents.

PATRICIA PRICE

Dealer in Quality Canadian Antiques and Folk Art
Since 1973

Visit our Shop & New Book Room: Drop by or call ahead

1320 King Street, R.R. 4, Port Perry, (Manchester) Ontario L9L 1B5

(Turn South at Rose Street)   **905-985-7644**

FRANKFORD
COLD CREEK COLLECTABLES
3 Trent Street South, Hwy. 33   K0K 2C0
613-398-6581
11-6 Saturday & Sunday
Plus holidays,
Other times by appointment.
Antique furniture, unusual iron,
Architectural & classic garden decor.

GLENARM
FRONT PORCH ANTIQUES & COL-
LECTIBLES
3658 Elm Tree Road   K0M 2B0
Debbie & Bryce Johnson, 705-374-5458
June-Oct. 11-5 Wed. thru Sat.; 11-5 Sunday;
Apr., May, Nov., Dec., 10-5 Fri, Sat., Sun.
Other times by chance.
Primitives, pine, original colour.
One of a kind unusual & handmade collectibles.

GOODWOOD
ELLEKE CLAASSEEN-VAN STEEN
R.R. #1   L0C 1A0
905-642-4755
By appointment only.
Specializing in Icons,
Fine 17th & 18th century
Furniture & accessories.

GOODWOOD
JOHN LORD'S BOOKS
Hwy. 47 at the Crossroads
P.O. Box 453, Stouffville   L4A 7Z7
905-640-3579
9-5:30 Tuesday thru Thursday,
9-8 Friday, 9-5 Saturday, 10-4 Sunday.
Antique and collectible books.

GOODWOOD
LAMB'S QUARTERS ANTIQUES
Hwy. #47 in centre of Goodwood
P.O. Box 67   L0C 1A0
905-640-4792
12-6 Friday, 10-6 Saturday, 12-6 Sunday,
12-6 Monday, or by appointment.
A general line of antiques,
Including Canadiana furniture,
Primitives & tools.

HALIBURTON
NANA'S AND PAPA'S
Main Street – Keith & Daphne Whiten
705-457-6695 / 705-754-1915 (res.)
1-800-434-1375
Victoria Day – Thanksgiving, 10-6, 7 days,
Antiques & collectibles, furniture,
English & Canadian pottery, china &
Cornflower glass.

HALIBURTON
OUT OF TIME
Hwy. #118, Box 628   K0M 1S0
Paulette & Mike Blake
705-457-4534 / 705-754-3883 (res.)
Victoria Day – Thanksgiving, open 7 days,
Rest of year: weekends.
Antiques & nostalgia, jewellery &
Furniture, country accents –
Rugs, cushions, etc.

HARCOURT
C&E ANTIQUES
Hwy. 648, off Old Harcourt Road
P.O. Box 101   K0L 1X0
Claire & Edward Loft
705-448-2550
10-5 daily, except Thursday
Oct. 1 thru June 30 by chance or appointment.
Antiques & collectibles.
Porcelain repair, furniture refinishing.

LINDSAY
J.W. HUMPHRIES ANTIQUES LTD.
9 Glenelg Street East   K9V 1Y5
John W. Humphries
705-324-5050
10-5 Friday & Saturday,
1-5 Sunday,
Other times by appointment.
Furniture & country accessories.
Member C.A.D.A.

LINDSAY
RIVERSIDE ANTIQUES
104 William Street North   K9V 4A5
Colin & Donna Campbell
705-324-1675
10-5 Saturday,
1-5 Weekdays, or by appointment.
Oak, pine, stained glass,
Nostalgia, telephones,
Clocks and toys.

LINDSAY
SECRET CACHE ANTIQUES
19 York Street North   L9V 3Z7
Opposite to the Legion
Gary Morrison
705-324-7350
See you at the shows, or
By appointment only.
Art glass, pottery, furnitue,
Decorative antiques.

LITTLE BRITAIN
COLONIAL CLASSICS CUSTOM
REPRODUCTIONS
R.R. #3   K0M 2C0
Ron & Monique Black
705-786-3262
Please call for directions.
Handcrafted furnitue – turn of the century
Ice box reproductions, ideal for microwave,
entertainment centre.

MINDEN
STOUFFER MILL BED &
BREAKFAST ANTIQUES
Halls Lake   K0M 2K0
Don & Jessie Pflug
888-593-8888
Antiques: At shows or by appointment.
705-489-3024
Country furniture,
Refinishing & restorations.

OAKWOOD
COUNTRY SAMPLER 1987
P.O. Box 100   K0M 2M0
8 Km. west of Lindsay on Hwy. #7
Jan Davie
705-953-9855
10-5 daily, 12-5 Sunday & Holiday Mondays
Antiques, country furniture & collectibles,
Folk art & gifts.

PETERBOROUGH
ANTIQUES AT THE BARN
Fowlers Corners at the Crossroads
Hwy. 7 at 7B (City Road 1)
705-740-2452; Fax: 705-740-0148
Website: www.roadshowantiquesmall.com
Daily 10-5
20,000 Sq. ft. of quality antiques.
Fine art, collectibles, memorabilia.
Operated by Roadshow Antiques, Cookstown.

PETERBOROUGH
DRAGON'S KEEP
270 John Street   K9J 5E9
Sheila Phillips, Errol Downey
705-876-9062
By appointment only.
Specializing in perfume bottles,and
Other unusual items.

PETERBOROUGH
LAST TANGO
374 Water Street North   L9H 3L6
Enter thru Planet Bakery.
Barb Connor & Chris Post
705-742-6510
Please call for hours.
Vintage clothing,
Antique jewellery,
Linens, textiles and ephemera.

PETERBOROUGH
LISA BEATTY VINTAGE LIGHTING
Peterborough   K9J 2A6
705-742-8078
http://vintagelighting.com
Major shows or by appointment only.
Vintage lighting, bought & sold.
Fixtures, sconces,
Floor & table lamps.
Restoration & polishing service.

PETERBOROUGH
QUEEN'S CROWN ANTIQUES
201 George Street North   K9J 3G7
Paul Bunn (Manager)
705-876-6409; Fax: 705-876-6317
9:30-5:30 Tuesday thru Saturday.
Quality imported antiques.
18th & 19th Century furniture,
Glass, porcelain, silver, brass,
Clocks, fine art, bronzes.

PORT PERRY
ANTIQUE & CRAFT SHOW & SALE
Scugog Arena
416-985-8840
Held annually in June
Sponsored by the Arena Board
60 booths to browse through.
Home baking available.

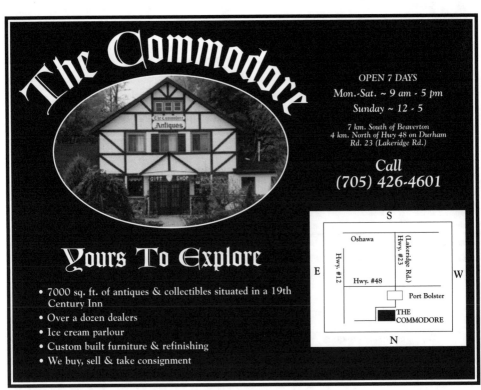

PORT PERRY
BETAL'S ANTIQUES & APPRAISERS
1 Lakeview Drive   L9L 1G4
B. & A. Lindsay
905-985-9391
E-mail: betalsantiques@sympatico.ca
Wednesday, Thursday, Sunday, & at shows.
Member: Asheford Institute of Antiques.
Certified Member: C.A.G.A.
Victorian furniture, buy & sell.

PORT PERRY
COUNTRY HEIRLOOMS
160 Queen Street   L9L 1B8
Sharon MacKinnon
905-985-8902
10-5:30 Monday thru Friday,
10-5 Saturday, 12-5 Sunday.
Antique & reproduction
Country furniture.
Old and new nautical.

PORT PERRY
THE GENUINE ARTICLE
223 Queen Street   L9L 1B9
Marlyn Rennie
905-985-4672
12-5 Sunday - Tuesday,
10-5 Wednesday-Saturday Call for winter hours.
Antiques, architectural details,
Design Elements
"From the Traditional to the Outrageous."

PORT PERRY – BLACKSTOCK
THE FRONT ROOM
3120 Hwy. 7A, 5 miles east of Port Perry
1 mile west of Blackstock   L0B 1B0
Merle Heintzman
905-986-5588
Daily from 10:30 a.m.
China, glass, primitives, furniture, etc.
In business 24 years.
No GST. Bed & Breakfast available.

PORT PERRY (MANCHESTER)
PATRICIA PRICE
ANTIQUES & FOLK ART
1320 King Street, R.R. #4   L9L 1B5
Turn south at Rose Street.
905-985-7644.
A call ahead is advisable.
Dealer in Canadian country furnishings,
Folk art, textiles, children's toys,
Some collectibles.
Since 1973

SUNDERLAND
THE GLASS GARAGE
48 Rive Street, P.O. Box 366   L0C 1H0
Denise Marsh & Ray Johnson
705-357-2476
E-mail: denise.marsh@sympatico.ca
Most evenings & weekends
By chance or appointment.
Furniture, glass, china, nostalgia,
Collectibles – Thinks unusual.

SUTTON
GEORGINA ANTIQUE MALL
& COLLECTIBLES
26602 Hwy. 48 (1/2 mile east of Sutton)
R.R. #2 Sutton West   L0E 1R0
Don & Bev Rintoul
905-722-6921; Fax: 905-722-8214
10-5:30 Daily April-Dec., 11-5:30 Thurs. & Fri.,
10-5:30 Sat. & Sun. Jan.-Mar.
Dog, horse & cat collectibles, books & music.

SUTTON
GEORGINA COUNTRY AUCTIONS
26602 Hwy. 48. (1/2 mile east of Sutton)
R.R. #2 Sutton West   L0E 1R0
Don & Bev Rintoul
905-722-9800
Monthly auctions – call for dates.

SUTTON
OLD MILL ANTIQUES
124 High Street
Box 1391, Sutton West   L0E 1R0
Mal & Valerie Ross
905-722-3227
Open year round.
Antiques, collectibles, primitives,
Antique lighting and
Country furniture.

SUTTON
REID'S ANTIQUES
20806 Dalton Road, corner of Baseline
P.O. Box 226, Sutton West   L0E 1R0
Ruth Reid
905-722-8200
11-5 Friday, Saturday, Sunday,
Or by appointment.
Antiques & collectables, furniture,
China, glass, costume jewellery.

Georgina
Antique Mall
& Collectibles

Doubled in size since opening in 1997

- 🐾 Over 30 dealers
- 🐾 5,000 sq. feet
- 🐾 New Merchandise Weekly
- 🐾 Over 3,000 Items
- 🐾 Collector Book Store
- 🐾 Furniture, China, Glass, Jewellery, Books, Pictures, Tins, Tools, Nostalgia, Toys, Crystal, Lamps, Dog, Cat and Horse Collectibles, and Much More

26602 Hwy. 48
(1/2 Mile East of Sutton)
R.R. #2, Sutton West, Ontario
L0E 1R0

(905) 722-6921
Fax (905) 722-8214

Don & Bev Rintoul

THE UNDERGROUND RAILWAY:
Canada's first refugee movement

Like many black Americans escaping slavery, Liza (Barbara Harris) is forced to endure separation from her family, clandestine travel and fear of re-capture along the route to Canada and freedom. This photo is from a scene in the Underground Railroad, one of many 60-second micro-dramas made for television by the CRB Foundation Heritage Project. NC

(NC) – No puffing steam engine ever rumbled down the tracks of one of Canada's first railways. No track linked it from one destination point to another. And no one ever used it for a carefree, leisurely trip.

Unlike most Canadian railways, it ran from south to north. During its short, 20-year history, it helped establish Canada's reputation as a haven for the oppressed. It was the Underground Railway, which of course, wasn't a railway at all but a code name for a network of courageous Canadians and Americans who helped 40,000 slaves escape from the U.S. deep south to freedom in Canada.

The "railway" operated from 1840 to 1860,, seven years before Confederation. Although Canada was then called British North America, it could be argued that the "railway" represented this country's first experience in opening its borders and hearts to refugees.

Back then there was nothing like a United Nations to help governments decide who qualified for refugee status. A country's ability to accept refugees depended on its people's willingness to support humanitarian efforts.

In what was then a British colony, private citizens led the movement to help runaway slaves settle here. Most who came settled in southwestern Ontario.

One such private citizen, Harriet Tubman, risked her own safety to become personally responsible for rescuing more than 300 slaves between 1851 and 1858.

She was a hero to the people in St. Catharines, where she based her operations. Her daring and successful sorties into dangerous territories inspired others to help runaway slaves escape to Canada. But in the United States, American slave owners placed a $40,000 bounty on her head.

People involved in the "railway" were known as "agents" or "conductors." They used barns and houses called "stations" to shelter slaves as they made their desperate flight to Canada. The "conductors" hid the slaves during the day and used the cover of darkness to get them to the next "station."

The "conductors" chose the routes carefully. It was often a cold and hungry trip through dense brush land, far away from travelled roads. The slaves could not light cooking fires as this might draw the bounty hunters to them. Few had a compass. Most followed the "drinking gourd" in the sky, the Big Dipper, to Canada.

Slavery had been officially abolished by the British government in 1833. The Abolition movement was also gaining strength in the United States. The movement received a severe setback, however, in 1850, when President Millard Fillmore passed the Fugitive Slave Law, making all escaped slaves subject to federal jurisdiction. They were denied both trial by jury and the right to testify on their own behalf, even in states where slavery had been abolished. Captured slaves were returned to their owners. Anyone caught harbouring a slave could be fined or thrown into jail.

Perhaps such repressive legislation inspired prominent Canadians to take very public stands against slavery. Civil rights champions such as George Brown, the Editor of the Toronto Globe, the precursor of the Globe and Mail, offered support through the Anti-Slavery Society. Newspapers of the day often carried stories about the inhuman treatment of slaves by their owners.

In 1850 the Governor General, Lord Elgin, gave a 9,000 acre site near Buxton, Ontario, to Rev. William King to establish a haven for slaves he had brought with him from Louisiana. This represented the main official act in support of the refugee movement.

Individual efforts on behalf of the slaves far overshadowed any government led initiative.

People like Harriet Tubman led the way. Their tolerance, compassion and bravery inspires Canadians even today, as we continue to welcome persecuted peoples from around the world.

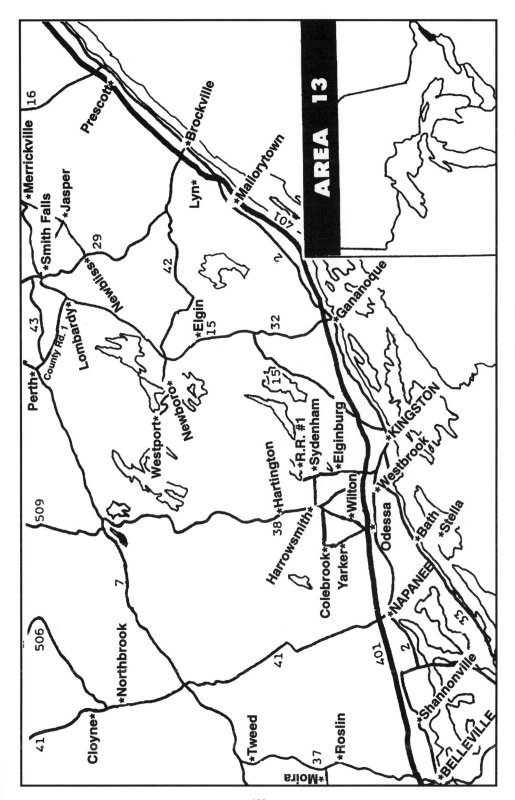

- 189 -

GREENBURNIE ANTIQUES LTD.

French Fruitwood Armoire, Normandy, circa 1820.
Subject to prior sale.

FORMAL AND COUNTRY FURNITURE IN THE GEORGIAN TRADITION. PLUS ACCESSORIES.

Paul C. Byington
R.R. 1, Lombardy,
Ontario, K0G 1L0
(613) 283-8323

Hours: Wednesday thru Saturday
10:00 a.m. to 4:00 p.m.

Canadian
Antique Dealers
Association

BATH
N.A. HAYNE POSTCARDS
& COLLECTIBLE PAPER
147 Church Street, P.O. Box 220   K0H 1G0
613-352-7456
E-mail: postcards@kos.net
Neil Hayne – by appointment daily.
200,000+ early postcards. Early prints,
Magazines, trade catalogues, view books,
Travel brochures, advertising & general ephemera.

BELLEVILLE
CENTURY ANTIQUES
225 Front Street   K8N 2Z4
9:30-4:30 Monday thru Saturday,
Closed Sunday.
1,600 Squar feet of quality antiques
& Collectibles.
We buy, sell & appraise.

BELLEVILLE
FUNK & GRUVEN A-Z
52 Bridge Street East   K8N 1L6
Mike Malachowski
613-968-5612
10:30-6 Monday thru Thursday
10:30-9 Friday; 9-5 Saturday.
Warehouse – Saturday only 10-5.
Period, antique and
Decorative furnishings.

BROCKVILLE
DOVETAILS & SQUARE NAILS
2857 2nd Concession Road
R.R. #1   K6V 5T1
Rod & Bea Slack
613-342-5223
Open by chance or appointment. All year.
Pine, oak, butternut furniture,
(Refinished or as found), quilts.
Coal oil lamps, linens, etc.

BROCKVILLE
STONE ACRE MANOR
Hwy. #2, east of town
P.O. Box 31   K6V 5T1
Hannah Jacobsen
613-342-4430
A call ahead would be appreciated.
Fine arts, bronzes, period furniture,
Porcelain, art glass, clocks,
Estate and antique jewellery.

ELGIN
MAINLY ANTIQUES
Main Street, Box 149   K0G 1E0
Prop.: Charles Marion
613-359-6324
10-5 Year round, closed Tuesday.
Antiques & collectibles in the Old General
Store. China, clocks, paintings, furniture,
Coins, glass, silver, etc.
Buy – Sell – Trade.

KINGSTON
CELLAR DOOR ANTIQUES
359 Barrie Street   K7K 3T2
Gary & Gayle Dawdy
613-546-7447 or 547-7800
Monday thru Saturday.
Gifts, antiques, unusual things.
Also home of:
Dip 'n Strip Refinishing.

LOMBARDY
GREENBURNIE ANTIQUES LTD.
R.R. #1   K0G 1L0
Paul C. Byington
613-283-8323
10-4 Wednesday thru Saturday
Formal & country furniture in the
Georgian tradition,
Plus accessories.
Member C.A.D.A.

LOMBARDY
RIDEAU ANTIQUES
R.R. #1, 10 miles west of Smith Falls,
8 miles south of Perth   K0G 1L0
Clifford L. Miller
613-283-6490; Fax: 613-283-6985
9-6 Monday thru Saturday.
Wide selection of general antiques,
Furniture, china, glass, clocks,
Woodenware & books.

LOMBARDY
OTTER CREEK ANTIQUES
"IN THE VILLAGE"
Mailing: R.R. #6, Perth   K7H 3C8
Bill Breeze
613-283-3161; after hours: 613-267-5040
May-Oct. 10-5; Tues. thru Sun.
Jan. & Feb.: weekends only,
Nov.-May 10-5 Thur. thru Sun.
Country furniture, nostalgia & artifacts.
Furniture restoration.

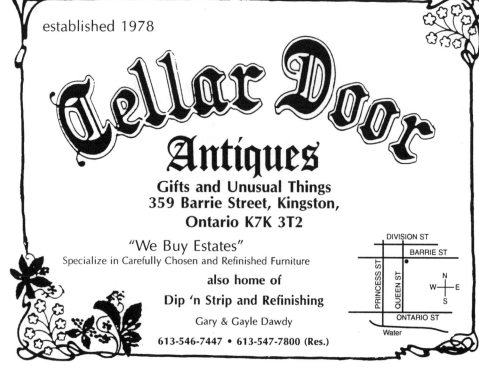

BROCKVILLE – MAITLAND
GRENVILLE MANOR ANTIQUES
1161 City Rd. 2. RR#1 Brockville   K6V 5T1
Robert Kwakernaak, Lesia Wood
613-498-4734. Fax: 613-342-3655
E-mail: grenville_manor@sympatico.ca
Summer hours:
9-5:30 Tuesday through Saturday
1-5:30 Sunday
A call ahead is always appreciated. Inventory
from several selected Eastern Ontario dealers.

NAPANEE
LENNOX & ADDINGTON COUNTY
MUSEUM
97 Thomas East, Postal Bag 1000   K7R 3S9
613-354-3027
10-4:30 Monday thru Friday,
1-4:30 Sunday,
Closed weekends November thru March,
& Statutory & Civic Holidays.
Displays, archives, genealogy pertaining
To Lennox-Addington.

NEWBLISS
FERNIE'S PLACE
#648 Highway 29
R.R. #2, Jasper   K0G 1G0
Donald & Carole Foster
613-275-1456 (bus.); 613-275-2608 (res.)
10-5 Wednesday-Saturday, 12:30-5:30 Sunday
"Antiques Homestyle", collectibles,
Special crafts, porcelain angels & fairies.

PERTH
COUNTRY LANE ANTIQUES
R.R. #3   K7H 3C5
Barb & Bruce Guthrie
613-267-4686
Best to call ahead.
Country furniture, refinished or
In the rough.
Unusual treen, decoys,
Goblets & Pottery.

PERTH
HALLETT ANTIQUES, Est. 1960
27 Leslie Street   K7H 2X5
Maurice W. Hallett
613-267-1182
Summer – regular hours,
Other times by chance or appointment.
Fine china, glass, silver, orientals,
Small primitives, Depression glass,
Unusual collectibles.

PERTH
PIONEER ANTIQUES
Jebb's Creek
2 miles from Perth on Rideau Ferry Rd.
Cal & Noella Richards
613-267-1145
Always open Saturday & Sunday,
Other days by chance or appointment.
Canadiana, coal oil lamps, crocks,
China & collector's items.

PORTLAND-ON-THE-RIDEAU
BYGONE DAYS
P.O. Box 187, Hwy. #15   K0G 1V0
Lois James
613-272-2800
Open daily July & August
Other times by chance
Or appointment.
Antiques, collectibles
& Nostalgia.

RIDEAU FERRY
LADY JANE ANTIQUES
R.R. #1 at the corner of
Rideau Ferry Bridge
P.O. Box 506, Perth   K7H 3G1
Dorothy Miller
613-282-8960
Shows only.

TWEED
BRIDGEWATER TRADING CORP.
Hwy. #37, north end of Weed
R.R. #3   K0K 3J0
Pat Lackie, 613-478-3255
24 May-Thanksgiving daily 10-5,
Other times Fri.-Mon. 10-5.
Furniture, nostalgia, jewellery, china, glass.
Antique market – collectibles,

WESTBROOK
BLANCHE LYNN
3448 Creekford Road, R.R. #1   K0H 2X0
Beverley & Blanche Lynn
613-389-1554
By chance or appointment.
A call ahead will be appreciated.
Canadiana, mostly furniture.

BRIDGEWATER
TRADING CORP.
Antique Market
multi-dealer

**COLLECTABLES ★ FURNITURE ★ JEWELLERY ★ ART ★ NOSTALGIA
RECORDS ★ CURIOS ★ BOOKS ★ CHINA ★ TOYS ★ AND MORE!**

WE BUY

WE SELL

★ Enjoy Our Super Malt Shop ★
Serving Breakfast, Lunches, Home Baking and Malts, Of Course!
Opens at 9 a.m.

7,000 SQUARE FEET INDOORS ★ SUMMER OUTSIDE DEALERS

M A R K E T   H O U R S
24 May to Thanksgiving:
OPEN Daily 10 a.m. - 5 p.m.
* *
All Other Times:
OPEN Friday, Saturday, Sunday
& Monday 10 a.m. - 5 p.m.
* *
CLOSED February

Market Located on Hwy. 37 at the North End of Tweed
R.R.#3 Tweed, Ontario K0K 3J0 Tel: 613-478-3255 Fax: 613-478-6061
For Dealer Space Call Pat Lackie at Number Above

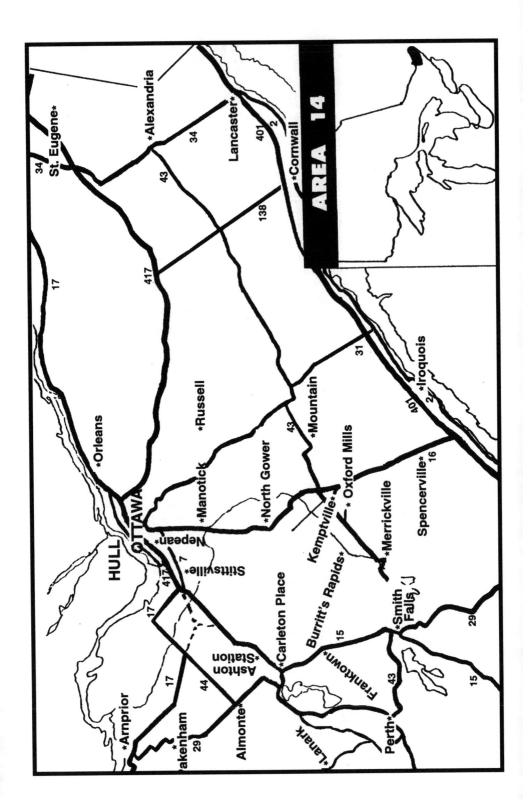

LAMPS REWIRED • BRASS POLISHED

ANTIQUES

HUGE
SELECTION
OF ANTIQUES

We offer...
Canada's largest selection of affordable authentic period lighting, thousands of fixtures, **shades** and specialty **parts**. Services include brass **polishing**, plating, **wiring** and **repairs**. We do large commercial applications, restoration, manufacture and design.

OPEN SUNDAYS

Yardley's
1240 Bank St.

Oak Furniture

739-9580
Fax: 722-0630

- Chairs
- Tables
- Stereo Units
- T.V. Armoires
- Bedroom Pieces

Early Pine

- Warm "aged" country colours
- Traditional finishes
- Choice of solid oak or pine
- Custom orders

TRUCKLOADS OF ANTIQUES WEEKLY!

WE BUY ANTIQUES

STONECREST ANTIQUES

Come and explore in our 1850's stone building.

Specializing in **Victorian & Canadiana** furnishings plus many collectables and a vast selection of antique fine china.

We're easy to fine. Just 12 km south of Carleton Place on Hwy. 15 in Franktown.

STONECREST
ANTIQUES & COLLECTABLES

	● Carleton Place
Hwy 7	
	● Ottawa
FRANKTOWN ☆	Hwy 15
Smiths Falls ●	
Hwy 401	
	● Kingston

We accept **VISA**
Tel: **(613) 283-1119**

The FOX & DUKE PUB and TEA ROOM

Fine English & Canadian Fare
Decadent Homemade Desserts

ALMONTE
FITZGERALD'S
7 Mill Street, P.O. Box 1670   K0A 1A0
Gabrielle Fitzgerald
613-256-2280; Fax: 613-256-9889
10-5 Tuesday thru Saturday,
12 noon-5 Sunday.
Antiques and art.
• Canadiana • Primitives
• Accessories and the unusual.

ASHTON STATION - LACHAPELLE
FURNITURE REFINISHING & ANTIQUES
Corner of #7 & Ashton Station Road
R.R. #4, Ashton   K0A 1B0
Gilbert Lachapelle
613-257-2960
Open daily.
Specializing in furniture.
27 Years refinishing experience.

BURRITT'S RAPIDS
ST. JOHN ANTIQUES
Country Road #2, Heritiage Drive
Box 284, Merrickville   K0G 1N0
John McManus
613-269-2967
Open by chance.
Pre-Confederation furniture
And accessories.

CARLETON PLACE
LOG FARM ANTIQUES
1563 9th Line Beckwith,
R.R. #2 Carleton Place   K7C 3P2
Bob & Shirely Kelly
613-257-3757
E-mail: rkelly@trytel.com
Open seven days a week
Furniture and accessories
Buy partial & full estates.

FRANKTOWN
STONECREST ANTIQUES AND
THE FOX & DUKE PUB & TEA ROOM
9619 Highway 15
Eleanor Placquet & Richard Carter
613-283-1119
11-5 seven days
Canadiana & Victorian furniture,
Fine china & collectables.

MERRICKVILLE
ARTIQUES FLORAL GALLERY
136 St. Lawrence Street   K0G 1N0
613-269-3199
10:30-5 Seven days.
Silk flowers, potted & hanging plants,
Garden furniture & accessories,
Wrought iron arbors, street lamps,
Victorian wicker chairs & tables,
Hand-painted furniture, mirrors.

MERRICKVILLE
KNOCK-KNOCK SHOPPE
117 St. Lawrence Street   K0G 1N0
613-269-4213
10:30-5 Seven days.
Quality antiques, Victorian-style
Reproduction furniture, Oriental screens,
Hand-made quilts, duvets, tapestries,
Blue & white ironstone china,
Framed decorator prints, photo frames.

MERRICKVILLE
SHADOW
211 Main Street West, Box 205   K0G 1N0
Roger Cloutier
613-269-2472
Website: www.collectable-antique.com
April 1 - December 24, 7 days,
January, February, March - weekends.
Antiques, collectables,
Sterling and fashion jewellery.

OTTAWA
27TH ANNUAL ASHBURY COLLEGE
ANTIQUE FAIR 2000
362 Mariposa Avenue,
Rockcliffe Park
Friday, November 3 - 6 p.m. - 9 p.m.;
Saturday, November 4 - 10 a.m. - 6 p.m.;
Sunday, November 5 - 11 a.m. - 5 p.m.
613-749-5954

OTTAWA
ARCHITECTURAL ANTIQUES
356 Richmond Road (at Churchill) K2A 0E8
613-722-1510
Regular hours
Vintage lighting and
Architectural accessories.
Brass polishing and
Lamp repairs.

OTTAWA
BANK STREET ANTIQUES
1136 Bank Street   K1S 3X6
613-730-0084
10-6 Monday thru Saturday,
10-5 Sunday.
Winter – shorter hours.
China, folk art, textiles, books, toys,
Fine and country furniture, glass,
Art Deco, Art Noveau, silver, quilts,
Clocks and watches and price guide books.

Ten dealers to fulfil your needs:
Barrie Whittaker,
Bizzare, Chronos,
Collectophile,
Ernest Johnson,
Guenter Dreeke,
Jane Mitchell,
Lionel Aubrey,
Margaret & Audrey Ruhland,
Nancy Allen.

OTTAWA
ERNEST JOHNSON ANTIQUES
292 MacKay Street
Mailing: Box 74026, 35 Beechwood Ave. K1M 2H9
Ernest Johnson
613-741-8565
Thurs., Fri., Sat. 10-5, Sun. noon-5.
Other times by appointment or chance.
18th & 19th Century furniture, European &
Canadian art, object d'art, silver.

OTTAWA
BLOOMSBURY & COMPANY
1090 Bank Street at Sunnyside   K1S 3X5
Tel./Fax: 613-730-1926
Don Patterson
11-6; closed Wednesdays.
Antique and period furniture, 20th century,
Silver, prints, china, pottery & decorative
items.
Always buying.

OTTAWA
DONOHUE & BOUSQUET
27 Hawthorne Avenue   K1S 0A9
Maint Street exit from "Queensway"
Lelia Donohue & Arthur Bousquet
Collin O'Leary
Tel./Fax: 613-232-5665
Silver, period furniture and porcelain.
Member C.A.D.A.

OTTAWA
LOGAN'S ANTIQUES
1097 Bank Street   K1S 3X4
Tom Logan & Dee Legault
613-730-8943
10:30-5:30 Seven days.
Specializing in art glass
& Art pottery.

OTTAWA
OTTAWA ANTIQUE MARKET
1179 Bank Street   K1S 3X7
10 minutes from Parliament Hill
David Smith, Manager
613-730-6000
10-6 Seven days.
Over 50 independent dealers.
Single items to estates,
Bought & sold.

OTTAWA
THE ANTIQUE SHOPPE
750 Bank Street   K1S 3V6
Robert and Graham Macartney.
Member C.A.D.A.
613-232-0840; Fax: 613-232-8308
10-5:30 Monday thru Saturday.
Broad selection of 19th century Formal and
Canadian furniture from England, Europe,
Canada and U.S.A.,Also eclectic mix of some
18th century & early 20th century.

OTTAWA
the CHINA CONNECTION
1181 Bank Street   K1S 3X7
Dina & Zilda Milne
613-730-3779; Fax: 613-230-5995
10-6 Monday, Wednesday, Thursday, Friday,
10-5 Saturday, 12-5 Sunday,
Closed Tuesday.
Antique Chinese furniture.

OTTAWA
YARDLEY'S ANTIQUES
1240 Bank Street   K1S 3Y3
613-739-9580
Seven days.
Antiques of all kinds, stained glass,
antique lighting, shades & parts.
Lamps wired, brass polished.
Antique garden accessories, mahogany,
Oak & pine furniture.

ᴀRTIQUES ꟻLORAL ꟾALLERY

- Gorgeous Silk Flowers • Swags
- Potted & Hanging Plants • Candle Rings
- Garden Furniture & Accessories
- Fountains • Sculptures • Planters
- Wrought Iron Arbors • Street Lamps
- Gazebos • Victorian Wicker Chairs & Tables
- Hand Painted Furniture • Mirrors
- Plaster Urns • Columns • Statues

Unique Floral Gifware

136 St. Lawrence Street, Merrickville, Ontario
(613) 269-3199
Open daily ~ 10:30 - 5:00

KNOCK - KNOCK SHOPPE

Quality Antiques • Victorian-style Reproduction Furniture

- Stained Glass, Crystal and Beaded Glass Lamps
- Large selection of hand-made quilts
- Wrought Iron Furniture & Accessories
- Fitz & Floyd and Blue and White Ironstone China
- Duvets • Tapestries • Throws
- Cushions • Deluxe Framed Decorator Prints
- Oriental Screens, Vases, Jardinieres
- Anne of Green Gables Dolls & Giftware
- Photo Frames • Clocks • Greeting Cards

117 St. Lawrence Street, Merrickville, Ontario
(613) 269-4213
Open Daily ~ 10:30 - 5:00

Donohue and Bousquet

ANTIQUE SILVER

subject to prior sale

A pair of German silver candlesticks in
the neo-classical taste made by Johan
Alois Seethaler, master silversmith,
Augsburg. Circa 1825.

27 Hawthorne Avenue,
Ottawa, Ontario K1S 0A9
Phone & Fax **613-232-5665**

Ernest Johnson Antiques

FINE PERIOD FURNITURE & ACCESSORIES
BOUGHT & SOLD

292 MacKay Street,
Ottawa, Ont. K1M 2B8

HOURS: Thurs. - Sat. 10 am - 5 pm
Sunday Noon - 5 pm

Tel./Fax: **(613) 741-8565**
Website: www.ernestjohnsonantiques.com

THE ASHBURY ANTIQUE FAIR

SIMPLY THE BEST!

27th Annual
Ashbury College Antique Fair
362 Mariposa, Rockcliffe Park, Ottawa

Dealers from Ontario & Quebec showing furniture, glass, china, clocks, estate jewellery, copper and brass, silver, textiles, carpets, maps, books, militaria, tools, lace and paintings.

2000 SHOW HOURS AND ADMISSION

Friday, Nov. 3	6:00 p.m. - 10:00 p.m.	$8.00
Saturday, Nov. 4	10:00 a.m. - 6:00 p.m.	$8.00
Sunday, Nov. 5	11:00 a.m. - 5:00 p.m.	$8.00
Senior (65+) & Youth (13-17)		$5.00
Weekend Pass		$12.00

LECTURE SERIES
Saturday & Sunday
(included in admission)

Tickets at entrance

DELICIOUS MENU
AT THE
ASHBURY CAFE

For information call 613-749-5954

OUT OF PROVINCE

MONTREAL
BEIM ANTIQUES
Sheilah & George Beim
1-800-267-2732
E-mail: belmantiques@attcanada.net
Exhibiting at major shows in
Ontario and Quebec.
Sterling silver flatware matching service,
Moorcroft, silver, porcelain and
Royal Doulton.

STE AGATHE DES MONTS
2 CONTINENTS
234 Rue Principale East   J8C 1K7
819-326-1235
11-5 Thursday thru Sunday
18th & 19th Century
European & Canadian antiques,
Furniture & accessories.

MONTREAL
HIDE-AWAY ANTIQUES
Aubrey & Frances
514-481-9059
Specialist in sterling silver cutlery, collectibles,
Brass, sterling, china, crystal, etc.
We buy & sell.
Exhibiting at major antique shows.
Please phone for details.

SASKATOON – SASKATCHEWAN
PAST AND PRESENT ANTIQUES
327 21st Street West   S7M 0W3
(corner of Avenue D)
Brian Hosaluk
306-242-9379
Fax: 306-653-5200
Open by chance or appointment.
Furniture, glass, china,
Vintage fashion, Art Deco, 1950s.

NOYAN
3 BELLES ANTIQUES
1070 3rd Concession   J0J 1B0
Katie & Bill Evans
514-294-3067
Open May to November inclusive, or
By chance or appointment.
Pressed & Pattern Glass Goblets,
Tableware & collectables.
Write for our listing of Pressed Goblets.

GREENSBORO, N.C., USA
REPLACEMENTS, LTD.
1089 Knox Road, Greensboro, N.C 27420 (USA)
1-800-REPLACE (1-800-737-5223)
8 a.m. - 10 p.m. daily,
Incl. Saturday & sunday.
3,000,000 pieces (60,000 patterns)
Of fine tableware and collectibles,
(Obsolete, inactive & active).
Over 900,000 customers worldwide.

SPECIALTY LISTINGS

Antique Malls & Co-Operatives

Antique Shows

Auctioneers

Services

Specialty Associations

INDEX TO DISPLAY ADVERTISERS

— *Notes* —

Great Books for Collectors!

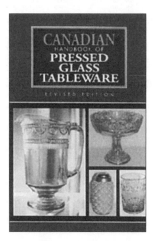

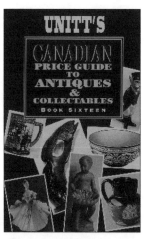